THE OCCULT PHILOSOPHY WORKBOOK

THE OCCULT PHILOSOPHY WORKBOOK
A One Year Course in the Secret Wisdom

John Michael Greer

AEON

First published in 2022 by
Aeon Books

Copyright © 2022 by John Michael Greer

The right of John Michael Greer to be identified as the author of this work has been asserted in accordance with §§ 77 and 78 of the Copyright Design and Patents Act 1988.

All rights reserved. No part of this publication may be reproduced, stored in a retrieval system, or transmitted, in any form or by any means, electronic, mechanical, photocopying, recording, or otherwise, without the prior written permission of the publisher.

British Library Cataloguing in Publication Data

A C.I.P. for this book is available from the British Library

ISBN-13: 978-1-80152-011-9

Typeset by Medlar Publishing Solutions Pvt Ltd, India

www.aeonbooks.co.uk

CONTENTS

INTRODUCTION   ix

UNIT ONE: The planes of being   1
  Lesson 1: What is occultism?   3
  Lesson 2: Spirit and matter   7
  Lesson 3: The inner life   11
  Lesson 4: The planes of being   15
  Lesson 5: The etheric plane   19
  Lesson 6: More about the etheric plane   23
  Lesson 7: The astral plane   27
  Lesson 8: More about the astral plane   31
  Lesson 9: The mental plane   35
  Lesson 10: The spiritual, causal, and divine planes   39
  Lesson 11: The path of evolution   43
  Lesson 12: The goals of occultism   47

UNIT TWO: Spiritual evolution   51
  Lesson 13: The cosmic planes   53
  Lesson 14: The solar logos   57
  Lesson 15: The lords of flame, form, and mind   61

Lesson 16: The elementals	65
Lesson 17: The mineral kingdom	69
Lesson 18: The plant kingdom	73
Lesson 19: The animal kingdom	77
Lesson 20: The human kingdom	81
Lesson 21: The mental sheath	85
Lesson 22: The two paths	89
Lesson 23: Beyond humanity	93
Lesson 24: The lords of freedom	97
UNIT THREE: Cycles of life and death	101
Lesson 25: The cycle of reincarnation	103
Lesson 26: The soul and the personality	107
Lesson 27: The first death	111
Lesson 28: The second death	115
Lesson 29: Heaven and hell	119
Lesson 30: The vision of the ideal	123
Lesson 31: Fate, will, and destiny	127
Lesson 32: Toward a new incarnation	131
Lesson 33: Reincarnation and the nonhuman	135
Lesson 34: The life and death of nations	139
Lesson 35: Ages of the world	143
Lesson 36: The cycles of time	147
UNIT FOUR: The way of occultism	151
Lesson 37: The sources of occultism	153
Lesson 38: Subjective and objective minds	157
Lesson 39: The process of occult training	161
Lesson 40: Seven spiritual laws	165
Lesson 41: The law of wholeness	169
Lesson 42: The law of flow	173
Lesson 43: The law of balance	177
Lesson 44: The law of limits	181
Lesson 45: The law of cause and effect	185
Lesson 46: The law of the planes	189
Lesson 47: The law of evolution	193
Lesson 48: The work of the occultist	197

ADDITIONAL LESSONS: The four gates of the year 201
 Additional Lesson 1: The spring equinox 205
 Additional Lesson 2: The summer solstice 209
 Additional Lesson 3: The autumn equinox 213
 Additional Lesson 4: The winter solstice 217

APPENDIX: Instructions for practice 221
 Discursive meditation 221
 Awareness exercises 226
 Affirmations 227

BIBLIOGRAPHY 229

INDEX 231

INTRODUCTION

The *Occult Philosophy Workbook* is an introduction to the basic concepts and teachings of contemporary Western occultism. While it is designed to accompany my book *The Way of the Golden Section*, and draws its teachings from the tradition presented in that book, it can be used equally well as a supplement to any other course of occult study.

Readers who set out to read this book from cover to cover in a sitting may find this a frustrating experience. As the title suggests, this is a workbook; it is divided into fifty-two lessons, each of which is intended to occupy one week of study, meditation, and practice. Approached in this way, it is the equivalent of a year-long correspondence course in occult philosophy, and will provide the student with a solid foundation for more advanced studies and practices.

You are not expected to believe the material in this book, or for that matter to disbelieve in it. Belief and disbelief are equally useless to the student of occultism. The teachings in this book are meant to train the mind, not merely to provide it with information; their goal is to guide you into an unfamiliar way of thinking, which will open many unexpected doors to you. The more time you spend pondering these teachings and working with them in meditation and other occult practices, the more effectively it will accomplish that task.

The main course of study in this book is divided into four units of twelve lessons each. The first, "The Planes of Being", outlines the nature of occultism and sketches the universe as it is understood in occult philosophy. The second, "Spiritual Evolution", sets out the process by which our souls have descended into incarnation on the material plane and what awaits us in the future. The third, "Cycles of Life and Death", focuses more closely on the process of reincarnation and on the cycles of history, which are simply reincarnation on a larger scale. The third, "The Way of Occultism", outlines the principles of occult practice and presents seven laws which can be used to make sense of the flow of events in the cosmos and in our individual lives.

Four additional lessons are included at the end of this book. These are not part of the four units just described. They have to do with the four gates of the year—the two solstices and two equinoxes, which are traditionally celebrated by most occult schools. Most calendars list the solstices and equinoxes each year, and you can also look them up online or in an almanac. Their approximate dates are given below:

Gate of the Year	*Northern Hemisphere*	*Southern Hemisphere*
Spring Equinox	March 21	September 21
Summer Solstice	June 21	December 21
Autumn Equinox	September 21	March 21
Winter Solstice	December 21	June 21

For the week in which one of these days occurs, study and meditate on the additional lesson for that date instead of the lesson you would otherwise be studying. It makes no difference where you are in the lessons; when your calendar shows you that the spring equinox will take place during the next week, set aside your scheduled lesson for one week, and work with the first additional lesson during that week instead. In the following week, go on to the next lesson in the unit you were studying.

Working with the course

As a workbook, this book is meant to be used as raw material for occult practice, not simply read or studied. The lessons are designed to be used for three specific exercises, and you may also practice any other occult exercises that are taught by the tradition or school you follow, or that you yourself have found useful. You may also find it useful to keep a practice journal, in which you take notes each day on the meditations and other exercises you have practiced.

The first and most important of the exercises to use with these lessons is discursive meditation, the Western approach to meditation, which trains the thinking mind instead of silencing it. Each lesson has been divided into seven numbered paragraphs, so that one of these can be used as a theme for discursive meditation every day during the week you spend on the lesson. Each lesson also has a diagram, which is meant to be used as an emblematic focus in the preparatory stages of those meditations.

The second exercise is an awareness exercise, which is intended to be done in spare moments over the course of your daily life. The third is an affirmation, which is intended to be practiced first thing each morning during the week you spend on the lesson. Both of these are meant to help you work with the concepts central to the lessons.

If you are unfamiliar with any of these practices, the Appendix gives detailed instructions for how to do them. You will want to read this section of the book and, in the case of meditation, work your way through the preparatory exercises, before you start work on Lesson 1 of this book. On the other hand, if you have already learned these exercises in the course of your occult studies, and especially if you start this book after completing the course of study set out in *The Way of the Golden Section*, you already know everything you need to know to get the most out of this book, and all you have to do is begin.

Students are encouraged to work through the lessons in this book at least three times, preferably with an interval of at least one year between repetitions. The concepts and images given here are capable of a great deal of development, far more than a single pass through the lessons will make possible.

UNIT ONE

THE PLANES OF BEING

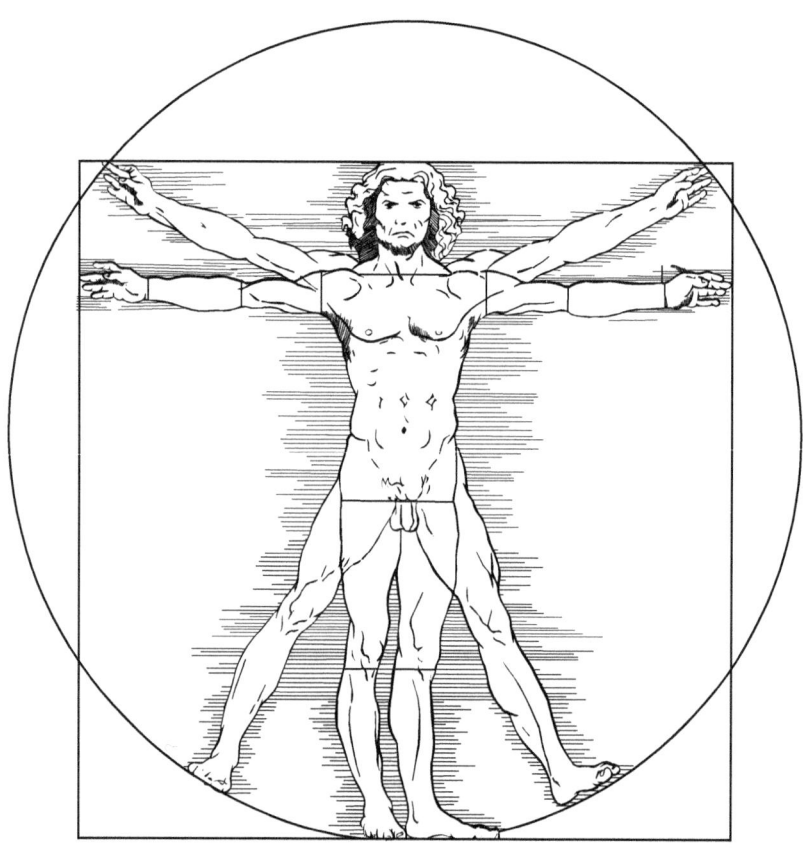

Leonardo da Vinci's famous Vitruvian Man, based on a traditional diagram of sacred geometry, represents the individual human being dwelling in the visible and invisible worlds at the same time. The square represents the visible world of matter; the circle represents the invisible world of spirit. The two worlds overlap, but not perfectly.

LESSON 1

What is occultism?

1. As soon as human beings first began to think about their experiences, they noticed that there were two kinds of things in the world. There were things they could see, hear, tap with a finger, and otherwise perceive through the physical senses. Then there were things they couldn't perceive by their senses, but could perceive by their minds either directly or indirectly. Their own thoughts, feelings, and sensations were things they could perceive directly. The thoughts, feelings, and sensations of other people were things they could perceive indirectly by watching the way other people spoke and acted. They could also observe the behavior of things that weren't human, which seemed to show that many other things in the world—and just possibly the world as a whole—also had thoughts, feelings, and sensations.
2. From the most ancient times, accordingly, human beings came to see themselves as dwellers in two worlds: one visible, the other invisible. To deal with the visible world, they devised a wide range of crafts and practical skills. To deal with the invisible world, in turn, they devised the earliest forms of religion, spirituality, and magic. With the growth of human culture, these two branches of knowledge and

practice developed together, providing our ancestors with increasingly effective tools they could use to deal with the two worlds that surrounded them.

3. As human beings learned more and more about the world known by the senses, certain things that once could be explained only by invisible forces found new explanations in the visible world. Omens that once tracked the cycle of the seasons were replaced by calendars; the art of healing, originally a branch of magic pure and simple, turned into a set of practical techniques based on knowledge of how the human body works; the sacred alchemy that drew shining metal from dull rocks turned into the craft of the blacksmith. (Most people have heard the story of how King Arthur drew a sword from a stone, but very few realize that this legend originated more than a thousand years before Arthur's time, in the days when drawing iron from ore was a secret of kings.)

4. This same process took a leap forward with the coming of modern science, when people found that many things once invisible could be brought into the visible world using the scientific method. When Isaac Newton realized that the same laws that governed a thrown rock also kept the Moon circling around the Earth, a vast number of questions that once belonged to theology became matters of practical knowledge. Scientists who followed in Newton's wake applied his methods more generally. Though the results were not always good, the success rate was high enough that many people came to believe that the visible world is all there is, and eventually everything would be understood by the methods of science.

5. What few people have realized is that the growth of scientific and practical knowledge about the visible world was paralleled by a growth of knowledge about the invisible world. One major factor in this parallel growth, ironically enough, was the growth of science itself. Once astronomy became scientific, astrology was able to develop independently. The same thing happened to alchemy once it separated from chemistry, and to natural magic—the study of the invisible influences of herbs, stones, and other natural substances—once the medical properties of these same substances became common knowledge.

6. In the nineteenth century, the word "occultism" was coined as a useful label for the body of knowledge and technique that relates to the invisible world. It developed from an older phrase, "occult

philosophy," which came into use in the Renaissance and is still used for the theoretical side of occultism. The word "occult" means "hidden"—it has no connection with the word "cult." When the Moon hides a star from us, astronomers say that the star has been occulted by the Moon, and health care providers use the term "occult blood" to mean blood that cannot be seen, but has to be detected by chemical testing.

7. Occultism is the study of the unseen. It is an extensive, detailed, and thorough body of philosophy and practice that deals with the invisible world—the world of thoughts, decisions, feelings, and sensations, and of the consciousness that experiences these things, in yourself, in other human beings, in other beings who are not human, and in the world and the cosmos as a whole. The teachings of occultism differ from some of the current beliefs held by authorities in the various branches of modern science. They also differ from some of the current doctrines of the various religions. In the long run, however, occultism, science, and religion are all compatible with one another, and the differences of opinion that presently divide them can all be resolved given mutual understanding and a willingness to learn from one another.

Awareness exercise

During the week you spend on this lesson, as you go about your everyday activities, notice the two worlds you experience—the visible outer world of things perceived by the senses, and the invisible inner world of things perceived by the mind. Pay attention to the differences, the similarities, and the interactions between these worlds.

Affirmation

"I dwell in two worlds—one visible and one invisible."

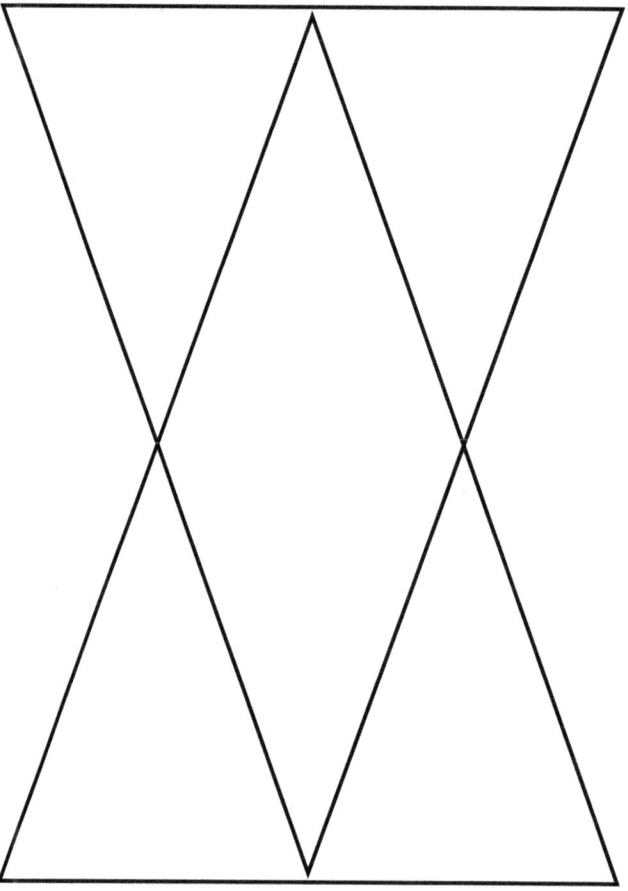

The relationship between spirit and matter, the two polarized states of cosmic root substance, is traditionally shown by two interpenetrating triangles, one descending from above to represent spirit, one ascending from below to represent matter.

LESSON 2

Spirit and matter

1. We can start exploring what occult philosophy teaches about the cosmos with the distinction between spirit and matter. This is not quite the same as the division between the visible and the invisible worlds discussed in the previous lesson, but the two distinctions are closely related. Scientists say that matter is the substance of the visible world, and occult philosophy agrees with this way of seeing things. Occultists also know, however, that there are substances that belong to the invisible world, and one of these substances is spirit.
2. Look at any object that happens to be in sight—this book, for example. Examine it closely so that you can see its details. Now, while still looking at the book, become aware of yourself looking at it. Pay attention, not to the book, but to yourself looking at the book. Be aware of your own awareness of the book. If you haven't tried this before, it may not be easy at first! Take your time, and get to the point at which you can slip from one to the other—from observing the book to observing yourself attending to the book. The book is a material object—that is, it is made of matter. The center of consciousness in you that perceives the book is a spiritual subject—that is, it is made of spirit.

3. Now consider your hand. You can examine your hand as though it was something not connected to you: you can look at it, poke it with a finger, and so on, just as you can with this book, or anything else in the visible world of matter. You can also feel your hand from within, experiencing other things through it and moving it however you wish. Again, take some time to do this, until you can easily move from experiencing the hand as a material thing to experiencing it as a spiritual thing, and back again. In this exercise your hand is sometimes an object and sometimes a subject—and sometimes both. It can do this, and so can the rest of you, because matter and spirit are both fully present in you.

4. Your hand is a material thing: you can see it, touch it, weigh it, just as you could do with most other material things. At the same time, your hand is not just a material thing. When you touch it, it feels the touch; the moment you want to move it, it moves. It is a spiritual subject as well as a material object, and it dwells in both worlds. This is true of you as a whole, and it is also true, according to occult philosophy, of everything else that we encounter in the visible world of matter. Whether we see it or not, spirit is always present.

5. One of the basic teachings of occult philosophy holds that everything in the cosmos is spiritual as well as material, and material as well as spiritual. In the heart of the densest material substance may be found the spark of spirit. In the heart of the most exalted spiritual beings can be found the seed of matter. Different things and beings in the cosmos have different proportions of spirit and matter. Human beings are among those roughly in the middle range, with spirit and matter more or less balanced within us.

6. Matter and spirit, as different as they seem to us, can interpenetrate in this way because they, like all other substances in the visible and invisible worlds alike, are forms of one original stuff, which is called "cosmic root substance". Matter is the most rigid and contracted form of cosmic root substance; spirit is a more fluid and expanded form of cosmic root substance. Put another way, matter is crystallized spirit, and spirit is rarefied matter.

7. In the visible world, matter surrounds you at every moment, but you don't encounter matter as such—you encounter objects made of different kinds, states, and combinations of matter. In exactly the same way, in the invisible world, spirit surrounds you at every moment, but as you learn to experience it more clearly, you won't encounter spirit

as such—you will encounter subjects (that is to say, living, conscious, intelligent beings) made of different kinds, states, and combinations of spirit. Behind all the objects you encounter in the visible world is matter; behind all the subjects you will encounter in the invisible world is spirit—and behind them both is cosmic root substance.

Awareness exercise

During the week you spend on this lesson, as you go about your daily activities, remind yourself that all the things you encounter contain both matter and spirit, in different proportions. Make an effort to think of the things around you as subjects as well as objects. See if you can begin to sense the subject in the object, whether that object is a stone, a tree, a dog, a human being—or something greater than human.

Affirmation

"In the heart of matter is the spark of spirit—in the heart of spirit is the seed of matter."

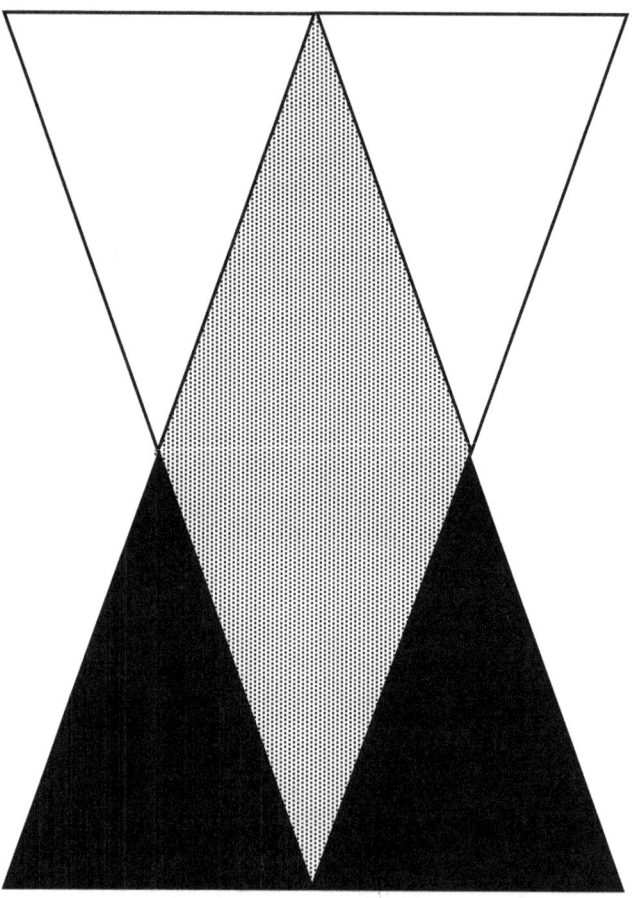

Between spirit and matter lies a range of other forms of cosmic root substance which can be experienced by human beings, some under ordinary conditions, some with special training. The region where they overlap is among other things the realm of humanity's inner life.

LESSON 3

The inner life

1. As we saw in the first lesson, occultism is the science of the unseen, the body of knowledge and practice that deals with the invisible world. Though we cannot use our material senses to perceive the invisible world, we have other ways to encounter realities beyond the visible world of matter, and one of the central goals of occult training is developing these other ways. Turning our attention inward, toward what we encounter in our own minds, is the easiest way for human beings to begin to perceive part of the invisible world. This is why it is the basis of meditation, the core discipline of occultism.
2. Turn your attention inward and see what you encounter in your own mind. Most people find it easy to notice certain things there, especially thoughts, memories, and feelings. Spend more time watching your inner life, and you will begin to notice other things that are also part of the invisible world, such as meanings, intuitions, dreams, daydreams, and much more. Many of these are things you encounter every day. The modern cultures of the industrial world insist that these exist purely inside your own head—but occultists know better.
3. According to occult philosophy, these things are also forms of cosmic root substance, like matter and spirit. Matter and spirit are two

extreme forms of cosmic root substance, and these other things fall in-between, not as crystallized and contracted as matter, not as rarefied and expanded as spirit. Just as all the colors of light fit into a spectrum that extends from red through orange and yellow to green, blue, and violet, all the things you experience fit into a spectrum that extends from matter to spirit and beyond. Your dreams, your thoughts, your memories, and your feelings are all forms taken by cosmic root substance. They are real, as real as things made of matter, but they have different properties because they occupy different points on the spectrum of being.

4. These other forms of cosmic root substance exist throughout the cosmos, in the same way that matter and spirit exist throughout the cosmos. They are not inside your head, any more than the things you see in the visible world around you are inside your eyes. Thoughts, feelings, intuitions, and dreams are part of the invisible world you inhabit. What modern culture calls "your mind" is actually a very complex set of processes that allow you to experience and shape some of these other forms of being, just as your physical eyes and hands allow you to experience and shape the visible world of matter.

5. This implies that you are more than a spirit in a body of matter. You are also part of all these other expressions of cosmic root substance. The usual way of saying this in occult philosophy is to say that you have more than one body. You have a material body, the body made of flesh and bone and blood you can see with your eyes and touch with your hands. You also have bodies of certain kinds of mind-stuff. All these bodies overlap, so that your body of matter is entirely inside the other bodies. You are in all your bodies right now, and the only reason they usually escape your notice is that you have been taught not to notice them.

6. All human beings have these other bodies, just as you do, and so do many other things that you encounter in the visible world of matter. This is the same thing as to say that all human beings, along with many other beings and things, have an inner life, a life lived in the invisible world of spirit. Different kinds of things and beings, however, differ in which of these other bodies they have, and thus in the quality and intensity of their inner lives. Stones have a very limited inner life, and they have only the undeveloped seed of an invisible body. Plants have developed one of their unseen bodies, most animals have developed two, and human beings (and a few other

creatures) are gradually developing a third. These differences show in the ways each of these things relate to the worlds around them, and to one another.

7. An important part of occult training consists of exercises to teach you to become aware of your other, invisible bodies, and the other bodies of the people and things you encounter. The most important of these exercises is daily meditation. There are other exercises that build on the foundation of meditation, however, to help you become aware of your other bodies. Every tradition of occultism has its own selection of such exercises, based on the experiences of its founder and those who have worked with the tradition during its history. What this implies, of course, is that there are many ways to accomplish the work that occultism does, rather than a single fixed path that all must take.

Awareness exercise

During the week you spend on this lesson, as you go about your daily activities, pay attention to the things you encounter, the things our society calls "living" as well as those it calls "nonliving." Notice how all these things interact with the world and with you. See if you can sense how much life and consciousness are present in each of them.

Affirmation

"Between spirit and matter are many worlds—and I am in all of them."

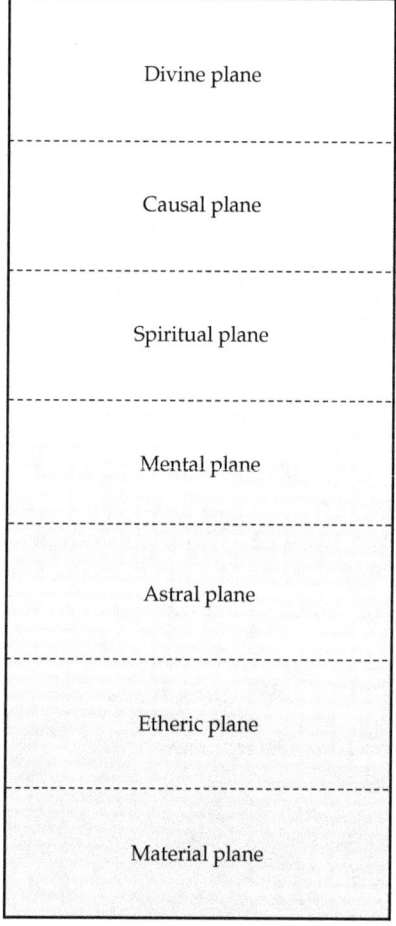

The seven planes of being are all forms of cosmic root substance, but they differ in their properties and characteristics. The planes are discrete and not continuous; influences can pass from plane to plane, but only where points of contact exist.

LESSON 4

The planes of being

1. The expressions of cosmic root substance that exist between spirit and matter can be sorted out into a set of realms, worlds, or planes of being. The various schools of occultism use different terms for these planes, and some of the schools draw the lines between the planes in slightly different places, just as the glow from a heater can be treated as light by one set of scientists and as heat by another. The general arrangement and the properties of the planes of being, however, are well understood by all.
2. We can consider the visible realm of matter as one of these planes and the invisible realm of spirit as another. For the sake of convenience, we can go on to speak of the material plane as the lowest of the planes, and the spiritual plane as one of the higher planes. These terms "lower" and "higher" are metaphors only; all of the planes of being are present in every part of the cosmos, and of course there is no up or down in space!. Experience has shown, though, that thinking of the planes as lower or higher helps the student of occultism make sense of them.
3. There are seven planes of being, though human beings can only experience four of them at this stage in our spiritual evolution.

Beginning with the lowest—that is, the densest and most familiar to us—the seven planes are the material, etheric, astral, mental, spiritual, causal, and divine planes. ("Causal," by the way, is not the same word as "casual"! The causal plane is the plane of causes, while the planes below it are planes of effects.) Each of the planes has its own distinctive properties and characteristics, and each plane must be approached from its own standpoint. Science works with the material plane. Occultism works with the etheric, astral, and mental planes. The spiritual, causal, and divine planes are the proper realm of religion.

4. Each of the planes has seven regions, which are different states or conditions of the substance of the plane. (They are not different places—all seven regions of each plane can be present in the same space at the same time.) In the material plane, for example, the seventh or lowest region is solid matter. Liquids belong to the sixth region of the material plane, and gases to the fifth; the lowest three regions thus consist of matter in the usual sense of the word. The fourth, central region includes radiant energy in all its forms, from radio waves through heat and light to x-rays and beyond. Gravity belongs to the third region, and subatomic forces belong to the second and first regions; the three highest regions thus correspond to what physicists call space-time. Every other plane of being is divided into regions in a similar way.

5. It is possible to have bodies on six of the seven planes. As a human being, you have a physical body, an etheric body, and an astral body, and so you can experience the three planes corresponding to these bodies. You are in the process of evolving a mental body, which will enable you to experience the mental plane; at present you have what occultists call a "mental sheath", which gives you glimpses of the mental plane only. You will evolve a spiritual body and a causal body only after long ages of further evolution, though there are beings in the cosmos who have them already.

6. While the planes form a spectrum of being extending from the densest forms of matter to the most exalted realms of spirit, the boundaries between the planes are important. A standard maxim of occult philosophy runs, "the planes are discrete and not continuous." The word "discrete" (not the same word as "discreet"!) means "distinct, separate, divided from one another." What this maxim means in practice is that things that happen on one plane do not necessarily

affect things that happen on another. There has to be a point of contact between the planes to allow influences to pass from plane to plane. Learning how to recognize these points of contact and how to work with them is an important part of occult training.

7. There are many different points of contact between the planes, but the one that will be most important in your occult studies is—yourself! Because you have etheric and astral bodies as well as a material body you can learn to experience the etheric and astral planes the way you now experience the physical plane. Because you have a mental sheath and are evolving it into a mental body, you can begin to catch glimpses of the mental plane as well. The world you can begin to experience as a student of occultism is thus even larger and more varied than the material world you already experience.

Awareness exercise

During the week you spend on this lesson, as you go about your daily activities, pay attention to the ways that the visible and invisible worlds affect each other. Notice how your thoughts and feelings shape and are shaped by your physical health and your surroundings. Try to notice where influences pass from one world to another and where they do not.

Affirmation

"I am a point of contact—between the planes of being."

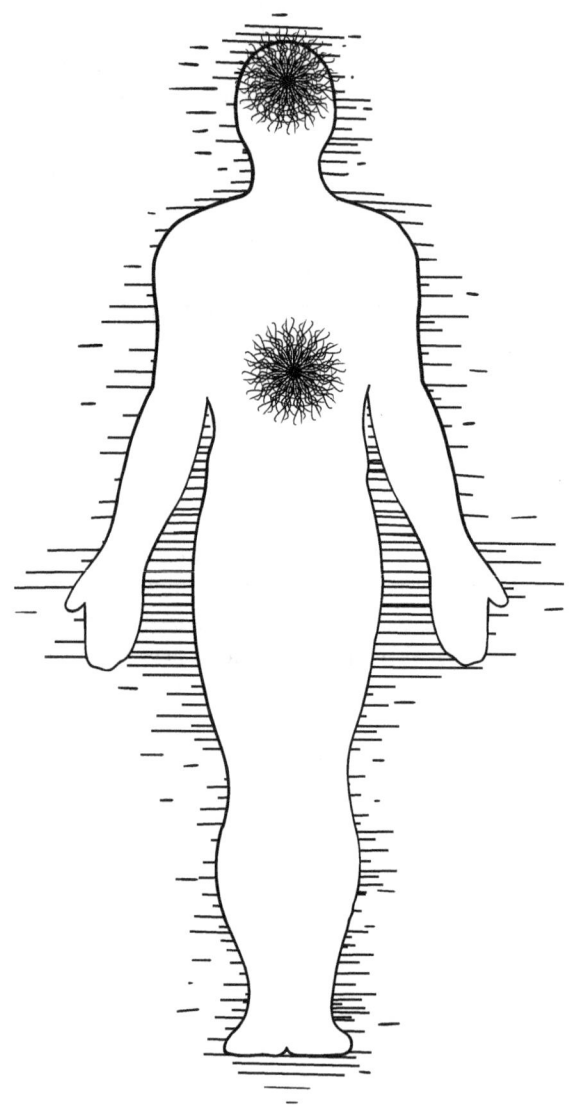

The etheric body is the body of life force. It fills the material body, flowing through the spaces between the material atoms, and extends a short distance beyond the skin. It contains 360 energy centers; the two shown in the diagram, the pineal gland and solar plexus centers, are central to the Golden Section Fellowship's work.

LESSON 5

The etheric plane

1. While the planes of being are discrete and not continuous, there are similarities between the planes, and planes that are next to one another are always similar in important ways. The etheric plane, the realm of being that is metaphorically just above the material plane, thus has many similarities to the material plane. Because of these similarities, beginning students often find the etheric plane relatively easy to understand, while the nature and functions of the higher planes tend to be harder for the novice to grasp.
2. The etheric plane is the plane of life-force. Ether, the substance of the etheric plane, is the basis of life. When a material thing has an etheric body, we call it a living thing—an animal or a plant. When the etheric body leaves the material form, we say that a living thing has died. Life on the material plane is the effect of etheric bodies acting on material bodies, and the more fully developed any etheric body is, the more of the properties of life it can express.
3. Things we call "inanimate" or "non-living" have no etheric body. Certain inanimate objects such as crystals, however, have an etheric sheath, a simple structure of ether that provides the simplest form of connection between spirit and matter, and which will eventually

become an etheric body after long ages of evolution. The creations of artists and craftspeople sometimes also have an etheric sheath, because life force flowed from the artist or craftsperson's etheric body into the creation, giving it a subtle life of its own. Many products of factories have no etheric sheath, which explains the dead feeling so many people sense from them.

4. All living things have a fully formed etheric body. The etheric body is the highest body possessed by plants, fungi, and simple living things such as bacteria. Some kinds of plants, such as seaweed, have simple and rudimentary etheric bodies; others, such as flowering plants, have complex and richly developed etheric bodies. Animals, which have another body above the etheric level, have brought their etheric body at least to the level of development reached by the most complex plants, and some have developed their etheric body much further than this.

5. Like every other living thing, you have an etheric body. Because souls who are born as human beings have gone further on the path of spiritual evolution than souls born as most other kinds of living things, your etheric body is extremely complex. It has two principal parts, the etheric double and the etheric aura. The etheric double, which is formed of the denser regions of etheric substance, occupies the same space as your material body, flowing through the gaps between material atoms, and extends out about a quarter inch beyond the surface of the skin. The etheric aura (also called the "health aura"), which is formed of the subtler regions of etheric substance, also occupies the same space as the material body and etheric double, and extends out several inches from the skin, depending on the health and vitality of the person.

6. The human etheric body contains 360 etheric centers. The seven chakras discussed by teachers of yoga are among these etheric centers. The *hara* or *dantien*, the center of energy in the belly used by many martial artists, is also one of the etheric centers. Each of the etheric centers has its own capabilities and powers. Just as different sports develop varying sets of muscles in different ways, each system of occult instruction selects certain etheric centers to develop in certain manners. This is why, if you read books on occult training, you will find different descriptions of where the etheric force centers are and what they do.

7. Ether, the substance of the etheric plane, also plays an important role in most systems of occult instruction, and in many other things as well. It has many names in many languages. Practitioners of yoga call it *prana*; martial artists call it *qi* if they practice a Chinese martial art, or *ki* if the art they practice comes from Korea or Japan; other traditions and cultures give it other names. It flows through channels in the etheric body, which are called *nadis* in the yoga tradition and "meridians" in the healing traditions of east Asia. When the flow is balanced and smooth, it brings health to the material body; when the flow becomes unbalanced and interrupted, it brings disease.

Awareness exercise

Rub your hands together briskly for a minute or two, and then shake your hands, as though you were shaking drops of water off them. Then bring them in front of you, slightly cupped, as though you were holding a ball eight inches or so across. Imagine a ball of light between your hands; breathe slowly and smoothly, and imagine the ball of light swelling a little as you breathe in, and shrinking a little as you breathe out.

As you do this, pay attention to the skin on the palms of your hands. After a little while you should begin to feel a slight pressure or tingling, as though there really was something between your hands. You are feeling your own etheric aura. Do this once a day during the week you spend on this lesson. As you go about your daily activities, try to feel your surroundings the same way you feel the pressure or tingling in your hands. See what you can perceive.

Affirmation

"I dwell on the etheric plane—and draw life and health from its tides."

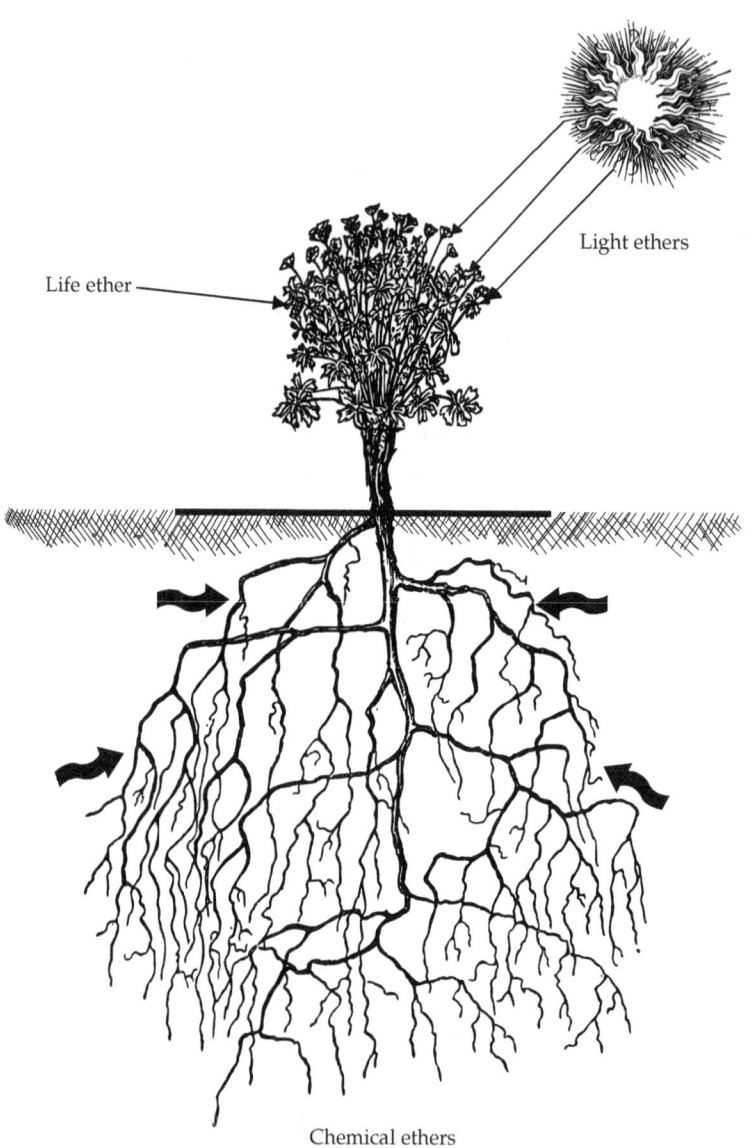

The etheric plane, like all the planes of being, is divided into seven sub-planes: three lower sub-planes that are of the nature of substance, a central sub-plane that is of the nature of energy, and three higher sub-planes that are of the nature of space. A plant shows each of these sub-planes in action on a small scale, but they are also active at much larger scales, shaping the activity of whole worlds and solar systems.

LESSON 6

More about the etheric plane

1. The etheric plane, like the other planes of being, is divided into seven regions, which are different states or conditions of etheric substance, ranging from very subtle to so dense that they verge on matter. As the material plane can be divided into three lower regions of matter, a central region of energy, and three higher regions of space-time, the etheric plane can also be divided into three denser regions of etheric substance, a central region of etheric energy, and three higher regions of etheric space. These are variously described in occult literature, but again, the basics are well understood by all occult schools.
2. The three denser regions of the etheric plane are called the chemical ethers, because they are the modes of the life force that work with the chemical substances of living bodies. They enable the roots of a plant to absorb minerals from the soil, just as they enable the digestive organs of an animal to absorb nutrients from food. They also give the body of a living thing the power to expel foreign substances and waste products, and to cooperate with other living things in the processes of digestion and excretion. The relationship of beneficial fungi with plant roots and of beneficial bacteria with the large intestines of animals are governed by these ethers.

3. The fourth, central region of the etheric plane is called the life ether. This is the ether that flows in and out of the body with each breath, and is used by healers of many traditions as well as by yogis and martial artists. The life ether gives the body its energy and vitality, and it also plays a central role in reproduction. It is the force that enables a plant to flower, set fruit, and bear seeds, and also the force that enables animals to mate and bear young.
4. The three subtler regions of the etheric plane are called the light ethers. As the chemical ethers connect the life force to the material plane, the light ethers connect the life force to the influences of the astral plane and the planes higher up. In living things, the light ethers are responsible for the circulation of sap in plants and blood in animals, and they help generate body heat in warm-blooded creatures. They also play an important role in the senses, linking matter and mind so that consciousness can experience what the material sense organs perceive.
5. The three regions of the chemical ether have the nature of substance, and so it is through the work of the chemical ethers that the soul builds a material body from solids, liquids, and gases. The life ether has the nature of energy, and so it is the ether of this region that governs the vitality of the body. The light ethers are of the nature of space, and they are influenced by the Moon, rising and falling in tides like the sea. This is why so many farmers and gardeners traditionally choose times to plant and harvest based on the phases of the Moon and the signs of the zodiac through which it moves.
6. The Earth as a whole is surrounded by an ocean of etheric substance in which all seven ethers are always present. As we stand on the Earth's surface, the chemical ethers are always flowing up toward us from a source at the center of the Earth, and the light ethers are always flowing down toward us from a source in the center of the Sun. These two flows have special names in occult lore. The upward flow from the heart of the Earth is called the telluric current (the word "telluric" comes from Tellus, an ancient name for the Earth) and the downward flow from the heart of the Sun is called the solar current.
7. Living things participate in both of these currents, drawing in the telluric current from below and the solar current from above, and participating in the chemical, life, and light ethers. Under certain circumstances, in individual living things or in certain other settings, the life ether can become the basis for a fusion between the solar and

telluric currents. When this happens a third current, which is called the lunar current, comes into being. The art of creating and directing the lunar current is one of the supreme secrets of practical occultism.

Awareness exercise

Walk on grass or bare soil, barefoot if the weather permits. Try to sense the telluric current flowing upward from the heart of the Earth. Notice whether you can still feel it through pavement. Another time, walk beneath the open sky when the Sun is shining, bareheaded if the weather permits. Try to sense the solar current flowing downward from the heart of the Sun. Notice whether you can still feel it when you are under a roof.

Affirmation

"I stand between the solar and telluric currents—in the place of balance and life."

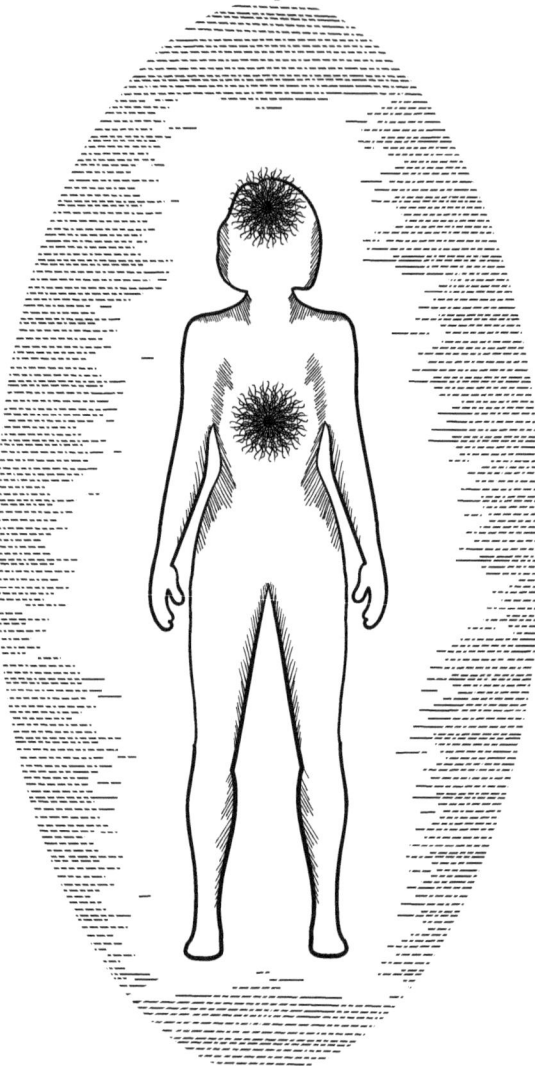

The astral body is the body of dreams, imagination, and feelings. Its outer layers form an ovoid shape surrounding the physical and etheric bodies. The more developed a person's creative and emotioal life is, the further the astral body extends from the material body. The astral aura is the part of the astral body outside the material body; many people can learn to see it, and most people sense it to some degree even without occult training.

LESSON 7

The astral plane

1. The plane of being that is metaphorically "above" the etheric plane is the astral plane. This plane is more familiar to you than you may realize, because desires, feelings, dreams, imagination, and most kinds of ordinary thinking belong to this plane. If you remember the face of someone you used to know, feel sad because the two of you are no longer in contact, daydream about what it would be like to get in touch with that person again, and then fall asleep that night and dream about that person, all these are astral experiences.
2. The astral plane gets its name because it is the plane through which most of the effects of astrology take place. Scientists have pointed out for many years that the other planets have only the slightest effect on our world. In terms of the material plane, they are quite correct, but the material plane is not all of existence. As the planets circle the Sun, they set complex patterns moving through the astral atmosphere of the solar system, and those influence all living things on Earth. Thus astrology is especially concerned with personality and interpersonal relationships, since these are so strongly influenced by the astral plane.

3. Inanimate things have no astral body, and neither do plants. Trees have an astral sheath, a simple structure of astral substance that over long ages will evolve into an astral body. All animals have an astral body, some more developed, some less so; the more fully developed an animal's astral body is, the more of the properties of consciousness it can express. Since the astral body is the body of feelings and ordinary thinking, those kinds of animals that have well-developed astral bodies also have feelings like yours, and can solve problems and do other tasks that require basic thinking skills.
4. Like every other animal, you have an astral body. Because souls who are born as human beings have proceeded further on the path of spiritual evolution than souls who are born in most other life forms, your astral body has evolved further than those of most animals, though it still has possibilities that you have not yet begun to develop. Your astral body has a set of 360 astral centers that correspond exactly to the 360 etheric centers of the etheric body. In most people, however, the astral centers are much less thoroughly developed than the etheric centers.
5. Like your etheric body, your astral body has two principal parts, the astral double and the astral aura. The astral double, which is made of the denser regions of astral substance, occupies the same space as your physical body and etheric double, and extends a few inches out beyond the surface of your skin, a little past the outer edge of the etheric double. This is the part of your astral body that contains force centers like those of the etheric body. The astral aura, which is made of the subtler regions of astral substance, fills a roughly egg-shaped region extending two to three feet out from your physical body in all directions. This is the aura that many psychics can see, and those who are experienced and skilled can read much about your character and your emotional state from the colors they see there.
6. The astral aura plays an important role in dreaming, imagination, and a great many other activities of your inner life. Its outer surface functions like a movie screen—but it is a screen that can receive images from both sides. When you imagine something, or simply think intently about it, you project the image on the outer surface of your astral aura, and it can be seen there by beings (human and otherwise) who have the gift of astral sight. When you dream while asleep, or simply clear your mind and allow images to surface, you are seeing images projected onto the outer surface of your astral aura

from outside yourself. Both these forms of astral seeing have their uses in occultism.
7. More generally, the astral aura is the interface between your astral body and the rest of the astral plane, including the astral bodies of other beings. Under some circumstances, you can influence how other beings think and feel, and they can influence how you think and feel. Psychic experiences such as telepathy happen through the astral aura. So do other experiences that seem much more mundane. Have you noticed that some people can improve everyone else's mood simply by walking into a room, while some people can make others irritable or unhappy without saying a word or doing anything on the material plane? These and many similar things work through the astral plane, as influences spread from one astral aura to another.

Awareness exercise

At least once every day, preferably when you are outside your home, clear your mind and try to sense how the space around you feels. If images come to mind, pay attention to them; if what you experience instead is simply a mood or a quality, pay attention to that. Do this for a few minutes, and then do something else instead. If what you sense upsets you or you have trouble shaking it off, eating food will help close down your inner senses.

Affirmation

"I dwell on the astral plane—and my inner senses are awake to its currents."

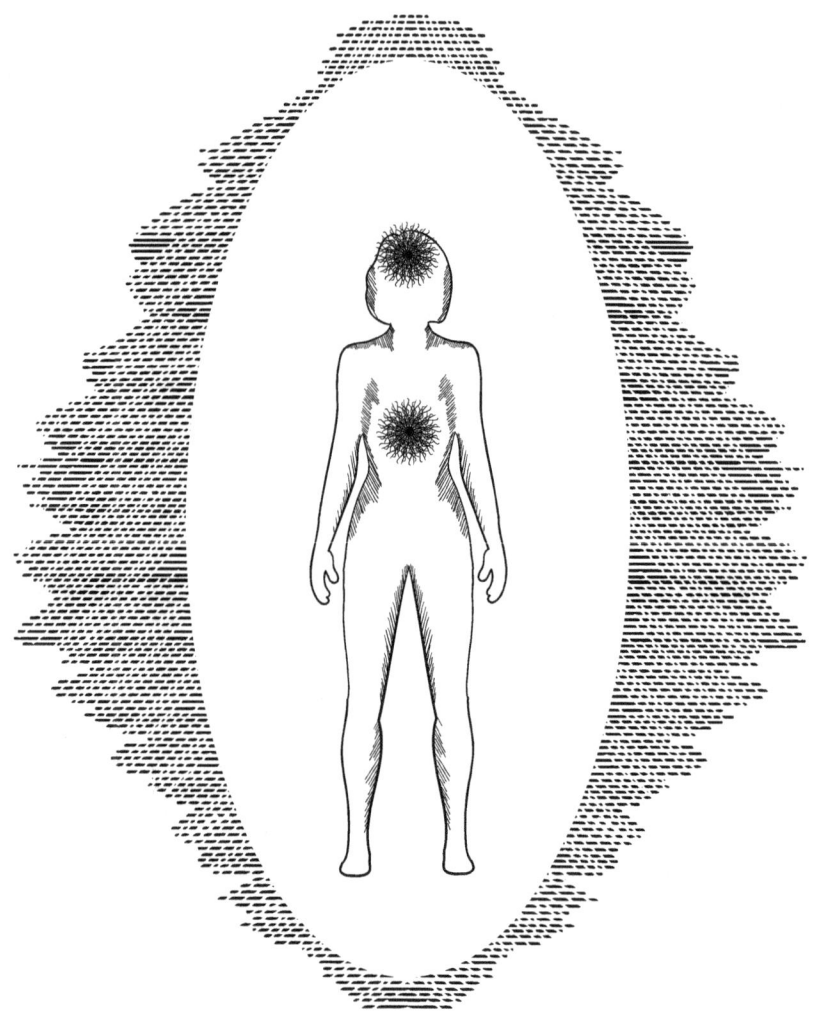

The astral body is surrounded by all seven sub-planes of the astral plane. The highest of these reflects the influences of the mental and spiritual planes; the lowest is the receptacle for corrupted and discarded forms; the others cover all conditions between these extremes. Your thoughts, feelings, and choices determine which of these sub-planes influences your astral body.

LESSON 8

More about the astral plane

1. The astral plane, like the other planes of being, is divided into seven regions, which are different states or conditions of astral experience, ranging from very subtle and clear to very dense and opaque. Like the regions of the other planes of being, the astral regions can be sorted out into three lower regions that resemble substance, a central region that resembles energy, and three higher regions that resemble space. These regions can also be understood as different kinds or qualities of thoughts, feelings, memories, dreams, and desires.
2. Each of the astral experiences just listed takes place on one of the astral regions. When you are asleep and dreaming, for example, the darker, more confused, more compulsive, and more frightening the dream, the lower its region, while the brighter, clearer, more lucid, and more joyous the dream, the higher its region. The terrifying nightmares that seem to take place in pitch darkness take place on the lowest part of the astral plane, while fully lucid dreams take place on the uppermost astral region.
3. In the same way, feelings, thoughts, memories, and desires that belong to the lower astral are murky and confused, and get in the way of clear thinking, while feelings, thoughts, memories, and

desires that belong to the upper astral are luminous and exact, and make it easier to think clearly. Those that belong to the middle astral fall in between. If you pay attention to the things that pass through your mind, you can learn to judge which of the astral regions your astral body is in tune with at any moment.

4. Occultists have worked out in detail which kinds of astral experience belongs to each of the regions. On the lowest or seventh astral region are the passions of the body, such as anger and sexual desire. On the region above this, the sixth region of the astral, are feelings and thoughts that are picked up from other people—for example, people who believe whatever they are told by the media, or by another person, are primarily active in the second astral region. On the fifth astral region are individual likes and dislikes, the things you desire or detest for your own reasons, not because your body reacts to them or someone convinced you to like or dislike them.

5. To the fourth, central region of the astral plane belong interest and indifference. When you pay attention to something without desiring or disliking it, or shrug and turn away from it, the fourth region is active. To the third region belongs personal feelings and thoughts—those that relate to oneself in some way, and include at least a trace of self-praise or self-blame. To the second region belongs impersonal, abstract feelings and thoughts, those that have no relation to oneself. To the first or highest region of the astral plane belongs creative thought and feeling: this is the region from which art, music, literature, and all other creative activities draw their inspiration, because it is closest to the mental plane.

6. Your astral body brings you into contact with all seven of these regions, but your own thoughts and choices determine which of these regions influence your astral body most strongly. The more attention you pay to the experiences of an astral region, the more strongly that region will influence you, and the more your own astral life—the life of thoughts, feelings, dreams, desires, and imagination—will be shaped by that region. This is why the teachings of occultism encourage students to pay more attention to the experiences of the upper astral regions than to those that belong to the lower astral regions—to thoughts and feelings rather than to desires and cravings, and especially to impersonal thoughts and creative inspirations.

7. This is important for the purposes of spiritual advancement in life, but it takes on an even greater importance at death. As we will see a little

later on in this course, the astral plane is the plane that determines what you experience after you die, and during much of the interval before rebirth. If your astral body is attuned to the higher regions of the astral, you can expect a much more constructive and pleasant experience after death than if it is attuned to the lower regions. This is the origin of conventional beliefs about heaven and hell.

Awareness exercise

During the week you spend on this lesson, as you go about your daily activities, pay attention to your own inner life. Notice how much of your time you spend on each kind of astral experience described above, and see if you can trace the way that attending to any given region of the astral plane tends to draw your inner life into resonance with that region and its typical states of consciousness.

Affirmation

"I attune myself to the upper astral regions—the realms of light and wisdom."

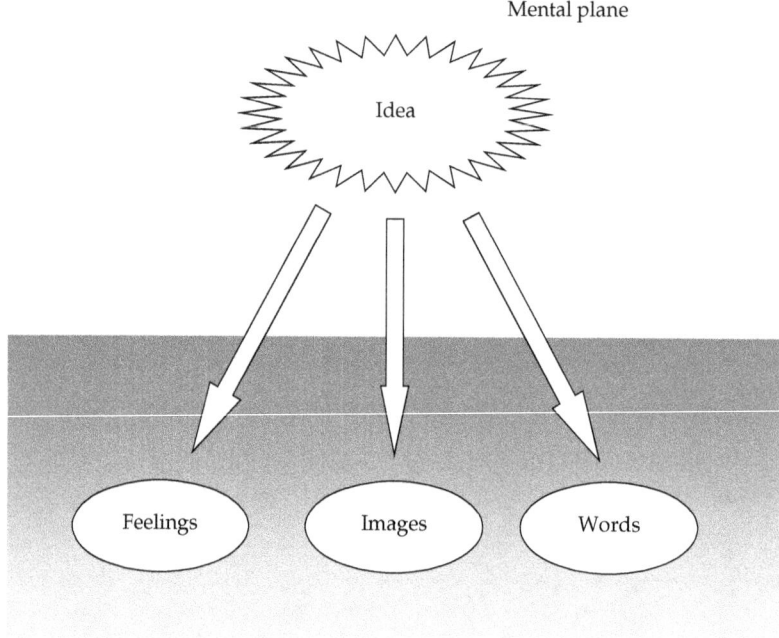

The mental plane is the uppermost plane of existence that human beings can experience at this point int their spiritual evolution. It is the plane of ideas—not of thoughts as we think them, but of the patterns of meaning those thoughts try to express. At first, we can only experience the astral reflections of the idea—the feelings, images, and words linked to that idea. As our mental sheaths develop, and begin to function as mental bodies, we begin to glimpse the idea itself.

LESSON 9

The mental plane

1. The next plane metaphorically upwards from the astral plane is the mental plane. This is the highest plane that we can experience at this stage of our spiritual evolution, and we can only experience it now and then, in an incomplete form. This is because we do not yet have mental bodies that can perceive and act on the mental plane, the way the astral body does on the astral plane, the etheric body on the etheric plane, and the material body on the material plane.
2. What we have instead is a mental sheath, a simple structure of mental substance that is in the process of evolving into a mental body. The mental sheath is what sets us apart from most of the animal kingdom. A few other living things, such as porpoises, also have mental sheaths and thus have inner lives and mental capacities comparable to ours. It also sometimes happens that an animal such as a dog or ape displays unusual mental powers compared to other animals of the same kind. This usually means that the soul of that animal has evolved a mental sheath.
3. All human beings have mental sheaths, but some have developed their mental sheaths further than others. To develop the mental sheath is to awaken the higher possibilities of the human mind.

To complete the process of evolving a mental body out of a mental sheath is to pass beyond the human level entirely, and to enter into a mode of being that differs from humanity as greatly as an animal differs from a tree.

4. To understand a little more about the mental plane, think about learning a word in an unfamiliar language. You can learn how the word sounds, how to speak and write it, and even how it fits into a sentence, and still have no idea what it means. Then you learn what the word means and the word stops being a sound or a collection of letters on paper. It turns into something else—a label for an idea. The sound, the spelling, and the grammar of a word all relate to the higher levels of the astral plane; the meaning relates to the mental plane.

5. Like the planes of being below it, the mental plane is divided into seven regions. Of these the three lower regions of the mental plane resemble substance, the central fourth region resembles energy, and the three higher regions resemble space. The human mental sheath can glimpse the three lower regions under ordinary conditions, and it can reach the fourth region in the practice of meditation. The three higher regions are the source of those transformative inner experiences that spiritual traditions call "enlightenment".

6. The three lower regions of the mental plane provide the insights and ideas that shape our thinking. The seventh or lowest region is the realm of forms, and we use this region to assemble the messages of our senses into a world of objects: we realize that this splash of color, this texture, and so on, all belong to a single object, a cup full of hot coffee. The sixth region is the realm of names, and we use this region to give names to objects: we look at a set of things and recognize that they are all cups, even though they differ in color and shape. The fifth region is the realm of functions, and we use this region to understand how things work: we look at cups, buckets, and bathtubs, and grasp the common function of containing a liquid.

7. These three lower regions relate the mental plane to things of the planes below it. To say the same thing in a different way, they relate the mind to the realm of objects. While the examples given above involve material objects, these lower regions of the mental plane also apply to things on the etheric and astral planes. On the fourth region, by contrast, the mind turns its attention back on itself. When we reflect on some idea—not simply experiencing it but thinking about it, pondering it, seeing how it connects to other ideas and how our

thoughts habitually deal with it—we rise to the fourth region of the mental plane. Done in a sustained and deliberate fashion, this is the secret of meditation.
8. The three higher regions of the mental plane are states of consciousness that human beings can only reach through the practice of meditation and other spiritual exercises. It is very difficult to talk about these regions in ordinary language. The fifth region, according to occult teachings, has the characteristic quality of bliss. The sixth has the characteristic quality of knowledge, and the seventh and highest has the characteristic quality of pure existence. Even with the help of meditation, we can experience these regions only in brief glimpses, but one such glimpse is very often enough to transform one's life.

Awareness exercise

During the week you spend on this lesson, as you go about your daily activities, pay attention to your thinking, and try to notice the difference between the astral reflections of ideas—the feelings, images, and words that pass through your mind—and the ideas themselves. See how often your thoughts and speech fail to express a meaning you can sense clearly.

Affirmation

"I rise to awareness of the mental plane—and glimpse the worlds of pure ideas."

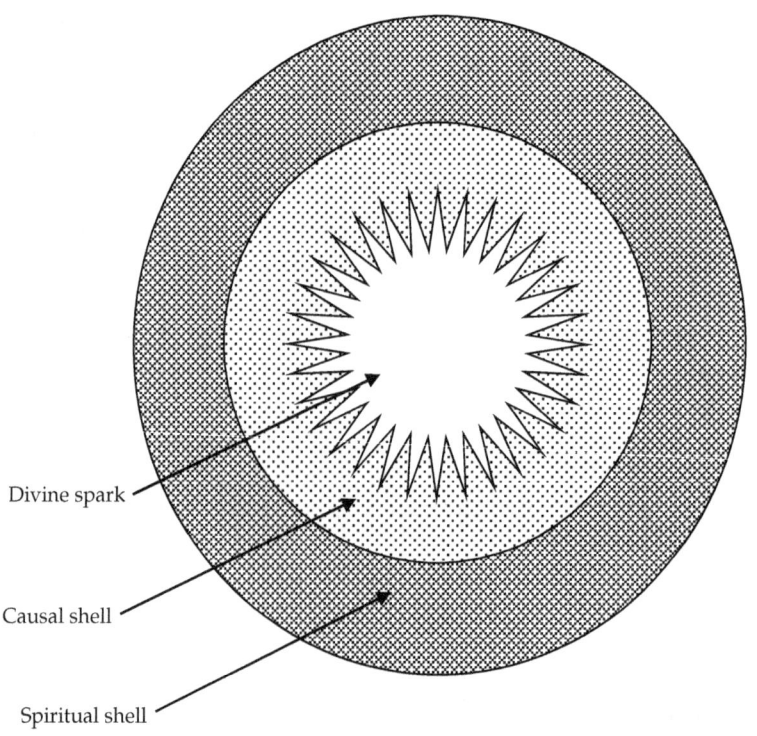

The soul of a human being consists of the Divine Spark, the essence of the self given by Deity, surrounded by unformed shells of the substance of the causal and spiritual planes. Before we reached the human level, an additional shell—the mental shell—was part of our souls. Ages from now, when we have finished evolving and elaborating our mental bodies, the spiritual shell will be transformed first into a spiritual sheath, and then into a spiritual body.

LESSON 10

The spiritual, causal, and divine planes

1. Above the mental plane, metaphorically speaking, are three more planes of being, which are called the spiritual, causal, and divine planes. While we are at the human stage of existence, we can know very little about these planes, and only after long ages of further spiritual evolution will we be able to experience them directly. What we know about them comes from encounters with Deity and with beings above the human level, and from glimpses that mystics have had of these higher planes of existence.
2. The spiritual plane, as explained back in Lesson 2, is the plane of consciousness, and you can begin to understand a little about it by thinking of your own consciousness. When you touch something of the material plane, it is the part of you on the spiritual plane that feels the touch. When you are aware of something on the etheric, astral, or mental planes, it is the part of you on the spiritual plane that has this awareness. We can talk about that part—the spiritual portion of yourself—as your soul. The soul is not limited to the spiritual plane, however; it includes the parts of you that exist on all three of the planes above the mental plane.

3. The causal plane, as mentioned back in Lesson 4, is the plane of causes, the level of existence of the original causes of all effects on the planes below it. You can begin to understand a little about it by noticing that your consciousness does not take in everything that surrounds you. You notice some things and not others, pay attention to this and not that, seek some experiences and withdraw from others. Habits you have established on the astral plane are responsible for much of this direction of consciousness, but behind the habits stands the basic direction and orientation of your soul, which occultists call the "true will". Your true will belongs to the causal plane. It is the part of your soul that seeks out those experiences that will lead you further on the path of spiritual evolution.

4. The divine plane is the plane of the Solar Logos, the regent of the Supreme Being in this solar system. At the center of your soul, however, is a little of the substance of the divine plane, which is called the "divine spark". The divine spark is not evolved by the soul, it is given by Deity, and it is the core around which all the rest of the soul takes shape. All the other parts of you—your true will, your consciousness, your mental sheath, and your astral, etheric, and material bodies—came into being to serve as vessels for the divine spark, so that it can exist, experience, and act on all the planes of being.

5. The nature and powers of the divine spark will not be unfolded within us until we complete the long pilgrimage of spiritual evolution and finish mastering all six of the planes below the divine plane. Until then it is simply a spark, surrounded by unformed shells of the substance of the planes we have not yet experienced, and bodies of the planes we have already mastered. Though it is only a spark, we are capable of experiencing it in one of its aspects, as the voice of conscience within us.

6. The souls of many beings who are not human also have a divine spark at their center. The soul of an animal, for example, is a divine spark surrounded by unformed shells of causal, spiritual, and mental substance, and the animal experiences its divine spark as the voice of instinct. The soul of a plant is a divine spark surrounded by four shells—causal, spiritual, mental, and astral—and the plant experiences its divine spark as the voice of *taxis*, the subtle prompting that makes roots grow downward and leaves turn toward the light. The soul of a stone is a divine spark surrounded by five shells,

and the stone experiences its divine spark as a single, wordless command: "Be."

7. Conscience, the voice of the divine spark in the human soul, is a transitional stage between instinct and a higher capacity, which is called intuition. As each human soul develops its mental sheath more fully, conscience begins to broaden out into intuition. What was at first a wordless sense of right and wrong, things that we should do and things that we shouldn't, becomes richer and more informative, a source of counsel and guidance in all the events of life. True intuition is always accurate, and so you can get some sense of how well-developed your mental sheath has become by noticing how often your "gut sense" of things turns out to be right as compared to how often it proves to be incorrect.

Awareness exercise

During the week you spend on this lesson, as you go about your daily activities, pay attention to your intuitive "gut sense" of what is happening around you and what you should do. Notice when that turns out to be right, and when you find out that you were mistaken. See if your intuition is more accurate on some subjects than others.

Affirmation

"At the center of my being is a divine spark—and I listen closely for its voice."

```
┌─────────────────────────────────────────┐
│                                         │
│              Divine plane               │
│ - - - - - - - - - - - - - - - - - - - - │
│                                         │
│              Causal plane               │
│ - - - - - - - - - - - - - - - - - - - - │
│                                         │
│             Spiritual plane             │
│ - - - - - - - - - - - - - - - - - - - - │
│                                         │
│              Mental plane               │
│ - - - - - - - - - - - - - - - - - - - - │
│                                         │
│              Astral plane               │
│ - - - - - - - - - - - - - - - - - - - - │
│                                         │
│              Etheric plane              │
│ - - - - - - - - - - - - - - - - - - - - │
│                                         │
│             Material plane              │
│                                         │
└─────────────────────────────────────────┘
```

The process of spiritual evolution begins on the divine plane and follows a descending arc to the material plane, where it begins an ascending arc back up to the divine plane. Souls pass through the descending arc in a subjective state, and achieve an objective state on the ascending arc.

LESSON 11

The path of evolution

1. Stones, plants, animals, and humans all consist of a divine spark surrounded by various arrangements of shells, sheaths, and bodies. The same thing is true of most of the other beings in the cosmos. The differences between them are a function of their current places in a process of spiritual evolution. This process begins on the divine plane, descends through the planes all the way to the material plane, and then ascends all the way back up to the divine plane. We can thus speak of spiritual evolution as comprising a descending arc and an ascending arc.
2. The descending arc of spiritual evolution begins when a divine spark moves down to the causal plane and gathers around itself a shell of the substance of that plane, becoming the simplest form of soul. Once that shell is fully formed and the soul has evolved certain capacities on the causal plane, the soul descends to the spiritual plane, gathers a shell of spiritual substance, and begins developing certain capacities on the spiritual plane. The process continues step by step down the planes, until finally the fully developed soul gathers shells of every form of cosmic root substance, completes the descending arc, and comes to rest on the material plane.

3. Souls make this descent in a subjective state. To understand what this means, think about the difference between ordinary dreaming and being awake. In ordinary dreaming, you are not conscious of yourself, and it never occurs to you to wonder at the strangeness of the things you experience. When you wake up, you become conscious of yourself, and the world around you excites wonder and reflection. Ordinary dreaming is a subjective state on the astral plane; waking consciousness of your thoughts and feelings is an objective state on the same plane.

4. In the same way, there are subjective and objective states of every plane from the divine plane down to the material plane. Each plane is experienced subjectively by the soul on the descending arc of spiritual evolution. In the course of its descent through the planes, the soul acquires a shell of the substance of each plane, and gains the capacity to develop the shell first into a sheath, and then into a body. The soul cannot make that capacity into a reality and create sheaths and bodies, however, until it completes the descending arc of its journey and reaches the material plane.

5. As it begins the ascending arc, the soul moves step by step out of its subjective state into an objective state. First it becomes objective on the material plane and develops a material body, existing as a material substance such as stone, water, or wind. Then it becomes objective on the etheric plane and develops both a material and an etheric body, existing as a plant. Next it becomes objective on the astral plane and develops material, etheric, and astral bodies, existing as an animal. After that it becomes objective on the mental plane, and the process continues.

6. In between each of these steps on the ascending arc is a transitional stage: a crystal develops an etheric sheath, a tree develops an astral sheath, a human being develops a mental sheath—and each of these proceeds to another mode of being as soon as the sheath becomes a body capable of existing in the objective state on its plane. As human beings, we occupy one of these transitional stages. Other beings reached our current stage long before we did, and passed beyond to higher modes of being. What we are now, they once were; what they are now, we will one day be—and when we have risen to those higher modes of being, souls that now indwell animals, plants, or material substances will be at the stage we inhabit today.

7. Thus vast numbers of the beings we perceive around us share the same origin, the same long journey, and the same high destiny. Stones, plants, animals, and spiritual beings are our sisters and brothers, part of one mighty family of souls. We all know this in our hearts, which is why so many of us feel strong bonds of affection with animals, plants, and the things of nature. Earlier in our own spiritual evolution, we have each been all these things. As Taliesin the Druid bard sang in his great song of triumph, "I have been all things previously." Each of us, when we awaken to an objective state on the mental plane, will be able to say the same thing, because we will have the same knowledge.

Awareness exercise

During the week you spend on this lesson, as you go about your daily activities, make an effort to think of everything you encounter as a being in the process of spiritual evolution, not simply an object. Think of yourself as surrounded by brother and sister souls in many different stages of the evolutionary process, all unfolding their potentials on the appropriate plane. See what difference that makes to the way you experience the world.

Affirmation

"I participate in the One Life—that binds all created beings together."

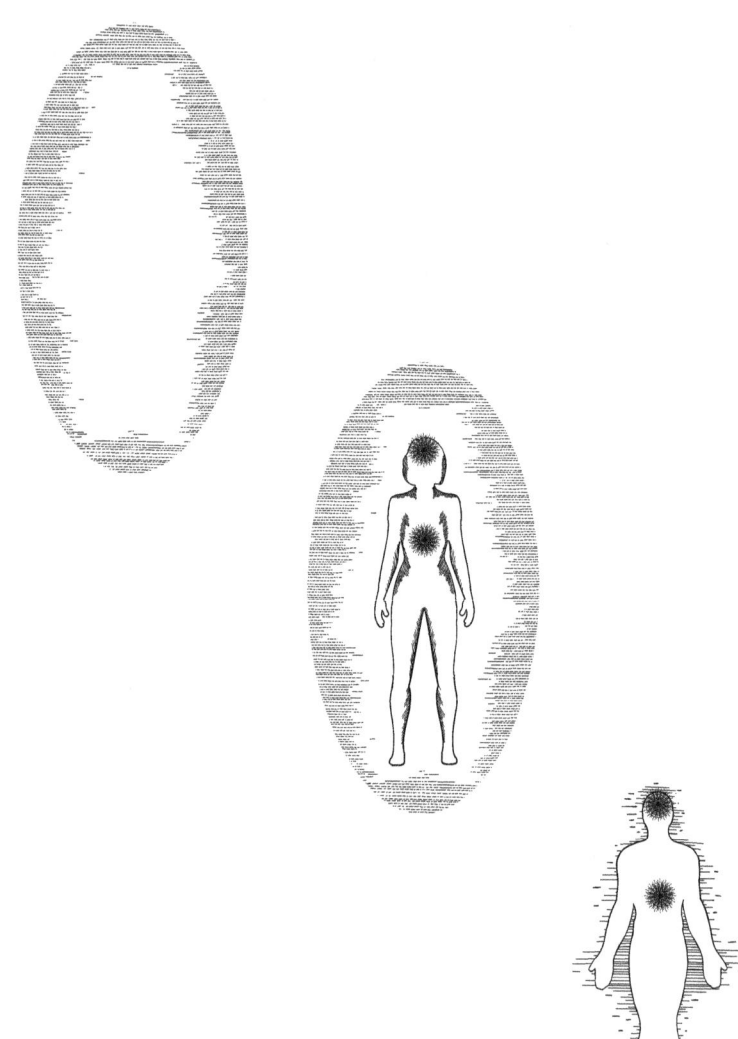

The etheric, astral, and mental planes, and their reflections on the human level—the etheric and astral bodies and the mental sheath—are the fields of activity to which occultism directs its efforts. The ongoing process of human evolution is taking place on these levels of being and in these bodies, and the occultist works to assist the evolutionary process, first in himself or herself, and then in the surrounding world.

LESSON 12

The goals of occultism

1. Occultism, as explained in the first lesson in this book, is the study of the unseen. It deals with the realities that exist between spirit and matter, the three subtle planes of being—the etheric plane, the astral plane, and the mental plane—that human beings can experience directly at this stage of our spiritual evolution. It thus stands between science, which works with the visible realities of the material plane, and religion, which reaches toward the higher, superhuman realities of the spiritual, causal, and divine planes.
2. Occultism thus deals with the planes where human spiritual evolution is at work. Our bodies on the material plane have been shaped and refined by countless generations of animal existence, and have remained all but unchanged across vast eras of human history: the people of the last Ice Age, who hunted mammoths for a living and whose vivid cave paintings of the animals of their time still delight viewers today, had bodies that were indistinguishable from ours. Our evolution on that plane is complete.
3. On the spiritual, causal, and divine planes, by contrast, we do not have bodies at all, and so we cannot yet begin to act and perceive on those planes. Even after we complete the work that lies before us

on the human level and our mental sheaths become mental bodies, long ages of further evolution will pass before we have developed all the potentials of the mental plane and are ready to begin to evolve a spiritual sheath—the first step toward the evolution of a spiritual body. Our evolution on these planes has not yet begun.

4. On the etheric, astral, and mental planes, however, we have work to do, and occultism teaches us how to do it. To study occult philosophy is to understand how we relate to the planes of being, how we have come to be what and where we are as human beings, and what further steps we can hope to take in this life and beyond it. To take up occult practice is to begin to take up the work of evolution consciously—to do in an intentional, deliberate fashion what each of us has been doing unconsciously, by trial and error, across the ages of time.

5. Our evolution on the etheric plane is almost complete. Our etheric bodies need only to be strengthened, cleansed, and charged with proper amounts and kinds of the chemical, life, and light ethers so they can finish going through the process of development in a natural fashion. Some systems of occult training use breathing and movement exercises to further this process; others simply advise students to take up an ordinary healthy lifestyle, so that their etheric bodies can finish their evolution on their own. Both of these are valid paths, though one or the other may be better suited to a particular person or specific modes of development.

6. The human astral body still has a great deal of evolution ahead of it, and the exercises taught in occult schools have the development of the astral body as a principal focus. In earlier phases of evolution, human beings developed the ability to function on the lower regions of the astral plane, but many of us still have difficulty experiencing and working on the upper astral regions. Meditation is of great importance in developing our connection with the upper astral, and so are other practices which link up the astral body with patterns of healing and blessing on the upper astral regions. However, anything that helps us learn to think clearly, feel fully, and imagine richly helps the astral body evolve.

7. The mental plane, however, is the cutting edge of human evolution, and this receives a great deal of attention in occult schools. As explained in an earlier lesson, human beings do not yet have a mental body—instead, we have a mental sheath, a very simple form made

of the substance of the mental plane, which will evolve into a mental body as we complete our work on the human level and prepare to go further. Meditation again is a crucial practice for developing the mental sheath, since it starts in the astral plane of thoughts and images and directs attention from there to the realm of meanings and pure ideas beyond it. Every time you devote ten or twenty minutes to meditation, you are traveling further on the road to higher modes of being.

Awareness exercise

During the week you spend on this lesson, as you go about your daily activities, continue the awareness exercise you did last week—make the effort to see everything you encounter as a being in the process of spiritual evolution. As you do so, however, be aware of yourself as one of their number. Approach your thoughts and feelings, your opinions and attitudes, as stages in a process rather than fixed realities. Imagine yourself looking back on them the way you now look back on the things you believed when you were a child. See what this does to the way you approach the world.

Affirmation

"I am journeying toward wisdom—with every passing moment."

UNIT TWO

SPIRITUAL EVOLUTION

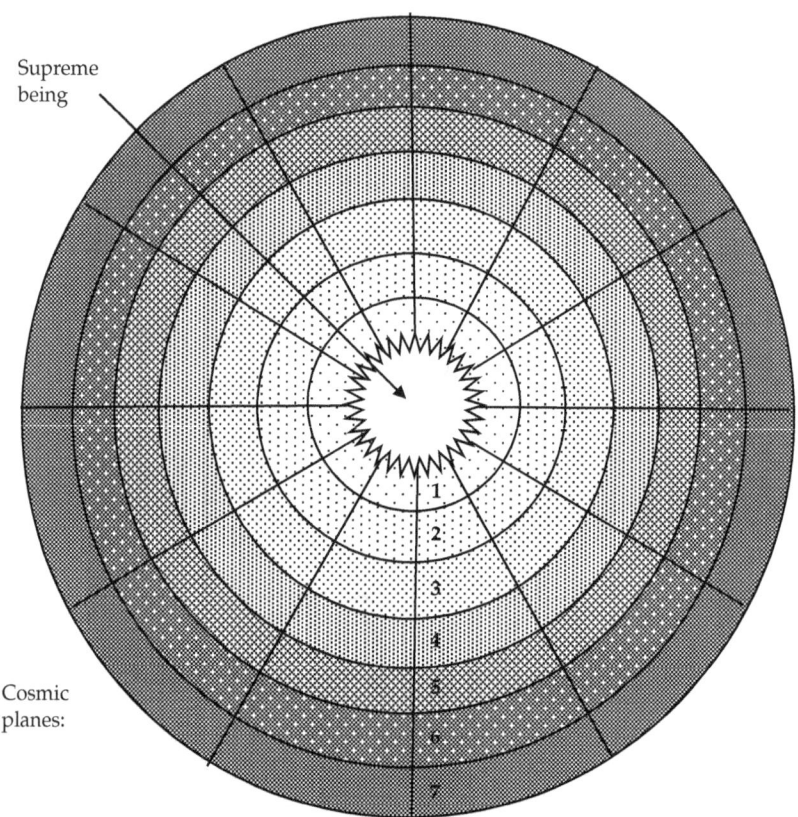

The seven planes that we can experience belong to the seventh and outermost of seven Cosmic planes. On each Cosmic plane are countless solar systems, each inhabited by beings of many different kinds. In this inconceivably vast cosmos each of us, and every other created being, has a unique place.

LESSON 13

The cosmic planes

1. The seven planes of being that have been discussed in previous lessons contain all that we are and all that we can experience. Our current condition as human beings, the states of being we have passed through in previous cycles, and the states of being we will attain when we have risen far beyond the human level are all included in those planes. For us, they are the whole of existence—but this is true only for us, and for other beings who dwell within our solar system and pass through the same process of spiritual evolution that we do. From another perspective, these seven planes are only a small part of a much greater cosmos.
2. The cosmos consists of seven cosmic planes, which are divided into planes the way the planes themselves are divided into regions. We exist on the seventh cosmic plane, and so does everything we experience—and everything we *can* experience. The seven planes of being discussed in earlier lessons, from the material plane to the divine plane, all belong to the seventh cosmic plane. There are six other cosmic planes, and each of them has seven planes of its own and beings who travel up and down those planes as we travel up and down ours.

3. At the center of the entire cosmos, above the first cosmic plane, is the Supreme Being. Occult philosophy has little to say about that mighty entity, for that topic properly belongs to religion, not to occultism. According to occult writings, the Supreme Being has three aspects, to which are assigned the characteristics of strength, wisdom, and beauty. With the Supreme Being at the center of the cosmos are seven mighty beings, the Seven Great Logoi, which some writings call "the seven spirits who are before the throne."
4. On each of the seven cosmic planes, solar systems come into being. We can think of them as circling around the Supreme Being at different distances, the way planets in a solar system circle around their sun. There are unimaginably many solar systems on each of the seven cosmic planes. All the stars in the heavens that have ever been seen by astronomers make up only a small portion of the solar systems on the seventh cosmic plane, and each of the other cosmic planes have roughly as many solar systems as the seventh cosmic plane does. It is possible that the solar systems on other cosmic planes, unseen by us but ever present, comprise the universe of "dark matter" discussed by today's physicists.
5. From the Supreme Being stream forth twelve rays, which pass out through the seven cosmic planes and influence everything in the cosmos. As solar systems circle around the Supreme Being, the twelve rays stream past each of them in turn, and the solar systems are influenced by the characteristics of the ray flowing through them. While a ray is affecting a solar system, everything associated with that ray becomes more active and important, and everything associated with the opposite ray is also strengthened in a more subtle manner.
6. This can be understood best if we remember that the twelve great rays are reflected in our solar system as the twelve signs of the zodiac. The great zodiacal ages known to astrologers on Earth—for example, the Age of Pisces and the Age of Aquarius, about which so much has been written over the last century or so—are the result of the rays affecting our solar system. It takes 25,920 years for all twelve rays to affect our solar system in turn, so that each age lasts 2,160 years. We are currently in the Age of Aquarius, which began in 1888 and will continue until the year 4048 AD; the previous age, the Age of Pisces, began in 272 BC and ended in 1888 AD, and the next age, the Age of Capricorn, will begin in 4048 and end in the year 6208 AD.

7. These sweeping perspectives of space and time are worth pondering, because they remind us of our own very modest place in the immensities of the cosmos. All the human beings who have ever lived and will ever live belong to one group of souls—one "swarm", as occultists call it—moving through a particular phase of spiritual evolution on one planet in one solar system on the seventh cosmic plane in an inconceivably vast cosmos. To ourselves, to each other, and to the spiritual beings of various kinds who concern themselves in our evolution, we are important, but we play only a very small part in the mighty drama of the cosmos.

Awareness exercise

During the week you spend on this lesson, as you go about your daily activities, try to balance the two viewpoints suggested in the seventh paragraph of this lesson—recognize that you are important to yourself, to other people, and to spiritual beings who have taken on roles in the spiritual guidance of humanity, and at the same time, remember that the cosmos is full of realms you will never encounter and beings who will never know that you existed. As you make this effort, see what it does to your sense of perspective about life.

Affirmation

"I am one small star—shining in an infinite cosmos."

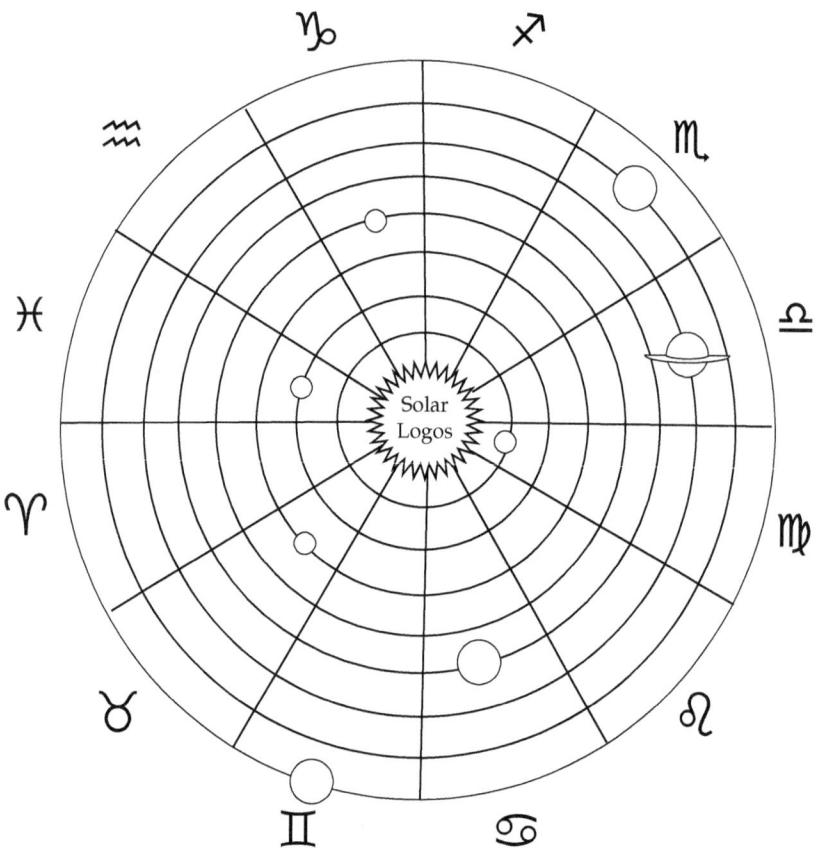

The structure of the solar system reflects that of the universe. The Solar Logos dwells in the center, the twelve zodiacal rays stream outward from there under the direction of the Star Logoi, and the planets circle the throne of the Solar Logos, each guided by its indwelling planetary spirit. Many smaller bodies also take part in the majestic dance of the solar system.

LESSON 14

The solar logos

1. Our solar system is one of countless solar systems on the seventh cosmic plane, as you have learned. Its structure mirrors that of the cosmos. At its center, where the Sun is located on the material plane, dwells the Solar Logos, who is the regent of the Supreme Being in this solar system and who dwells alone on the divine plane. Long before our solar system was born, in worlds that have long since ceased to be, the Solar Logos passed through the same process of spiritual evolution that we are passing through now. The task of the Solar Logos is to guide this solar system and the souls within it, and to mediate the forces of the cosmos for their benefit.
2. Just as the twelve cosmic rays stream out from the Supreme Being to influence all the solar systems on the seven cosmic planes, twelve rays stream out from the Solar Logos. These are called the signs of the zodiac. Just as each solar system circling the Supreme Being passes through all the cosmic rays in turn, each planet in our solar system passes through each of the signs of the zodiac as it circles the Sun. Each sign has its own nature and influence, and affects the planets as they pass through it in their orbits.

3. Each of the signs of the zodiac in our solar system has a great spiritual being to mediate its influence in the solar system. These beings are the twelve Star Logoi. They also went through the process of spiritual evolution long ages ago, but they are subordinate to the Solar Logos and dwell on the causal plane. They work together under the guidance of the Solar Logos to maintain the balance of the solar system and assist the evolution of the souls within it. Each planet in the solar system was created with the help of one of the Star Logoi and still has a potent spiritual connection to the sign ruled by that Logos. Astrologers describe this by saying that each planet is exalted in one of the signs of the zodiac.

4. There are eight planets in our solar system—Mercury, Venus, Earth, Mars, Jupiter, Saturn, Uranus, and Neptune. There are also many smaller bodies, including dwarf planets, asteroids, and comets. The Moon is a dwarf planet, like Ceres and Pluto, but it affects the Earth like a full planet because it is so close to us. The other dwarf planets and smaller bodies have less obvious effects on Earth, but everything in the solar system is interconnected and affects everything else. This constant interconnection between all things is what gives astrology and other occult practices the power to have the results they do.

5. Each planet and each dwarf planet has a Planetary Spirit, a great spiritual being who indwells the material planet the way humans indwell their material bodies. The Planetary Spirits did not come into being through the descent of a divine spark through the planes of being, and they do not pass through the same kind of spiritual evolution we do. As we will discuss in a later lesson, they evolve by sharing in the experiences of the souls who dwell on their planet. The being that many people call Gaia or Mother Nature is the Planetary Spirit of the Earth. Dwarf planets and smaller bodies also have spirits of this kind, but they have a different destiny, since their material bodies do not normally have souls living on them and so their Planetary Spirits do not evolve in the same way.

6. Each planet has countless souls dwelling on it, just as our Earth does. At this stage of the evolution of the solar system, however, Earth is the only planet in our solar system in which souls take on living bodies of dense material substances like ours. The Planetary Spirit of the Earth is therefore of special importance in our evolution, and is assisted by the Spirit of the Moon, who also helps guide us. In the distant past, when the Sun was smaller and cooler than it is now,

Venus was the planet where souls took on living bodies like ours. In the far future, when the Sun will be larger and hotter than it is now, Mars will have the same role.

7. Souls on every planet in the solar system, however, are passing through some equivalent of the same process of spiritual evolution as humanity. In one way or another, these souls descend through the planes in a subjective condition, waken to objective existence on the lowest plane, and then ascend through the planes again, gaining mastery over the possibilities open to them on each plane in turn. When they have completed this process they go on to other modes of existence in the solar system.

Awareness exercise

During the week you spend on this lesson, as you go about your daily activities, try to think of the solar system around you in the terms described above. Think of the Sun as the dwelling and material body of the Solar Logos, of the Earth as the dwelling and material body of a Planetary Spirit, of the Moon as the dwelling and material body of a different kind of spirit, and of the solar system around you as a realm full of many different kinds of life and intelligence.

Affirmation

"I dwell in a solar system—full of life and wisdom."

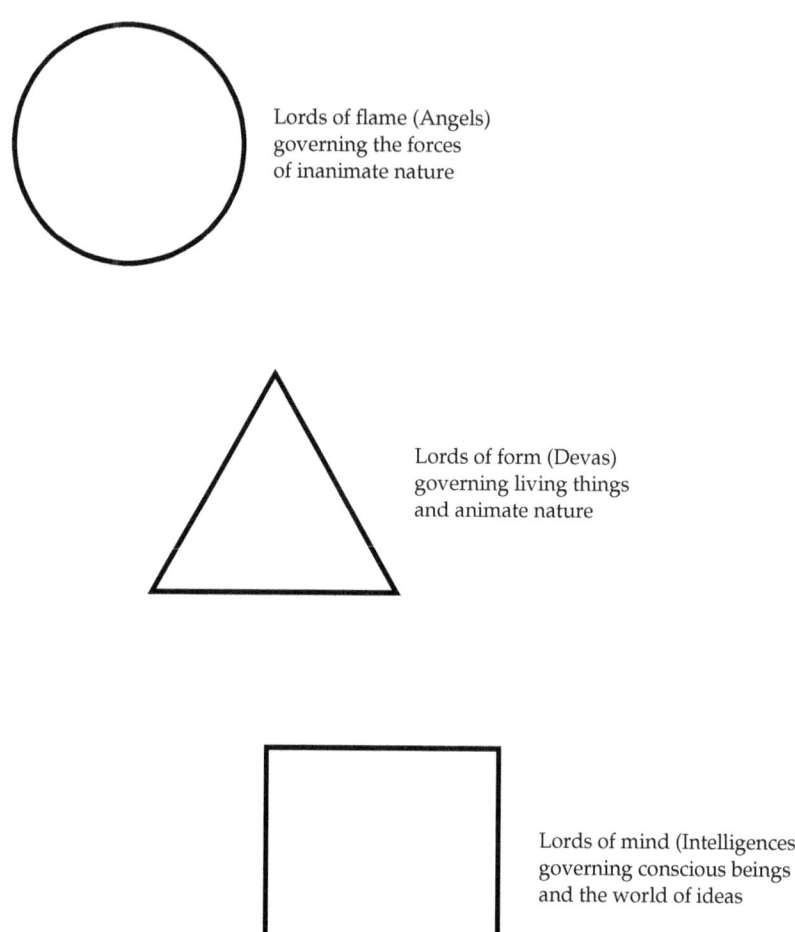

The three primal swarms—the Lords of Flame, Form, and Mind—passed through the process of spiritual evolution long ages before our swarm began its journey down the planes. Having completed their journey, they now serve the Solar Logos in various ways according to the capacities they evolved in their journeys down and back up the planes. When humanity has finished a comparable journey, we will become a fourth set of servants of the Logos.

LESSON 15

The lords of flame, form, and mind

1. Our solar system in its present form has been in existence for more than four billion years. During that time three great swarms of souls have completed the long journey down from the divine plane to the material plane and back up to the divine plane. A fourth swarm, the one to which we belong, is in the middle of the same journey. After our swarm has completed its journey, three more swarms will make the same pilgrimage before the life cycle of our solar system is complete and a new cycle begins.
2. The three swarms who have already completed the journey are called the Lords of Flame, the Lords of Form, and the Lords of Mind. Having completed their own spiritual evolution and achieved levels of strength, wisdom, and beauty far beyond anything we can even imagine, they serve the Solar Logos in ways suited to their capacities. Each of the three primal swarms has another name: the Lords of Flame are also called "angels", the Lords of Form are also called "devas", and the Lords of Mind are also called "intelligences".
3. The swarm that eventually became the Lords of Flame began its pilgrimage through the planes in the earliest days of the solar system, when nothing existed in this part of the seventh cosmic plane but

a vast, slowly spinning cloud of dust. By their lives and labors, the members of the first swarm drew the dust cloud together into an ordered solar system of a sun, eight planets, and many smaller bodies, and then kindled the fire of the Sun to light the habitation of the Solar Logos. Today they are pure disembodied spirits, and are responsible for those patterns of action and reaction that we call the laws of physics and astronomy.

4. The swarm that eventually became the Lords of Form began its pilgrimage after the Lords of Flame had completed theirs, when the Sun was newborn and his eight planets were still smoldering masses of red-hot rock on which life had not yet emerged. By their lives and labors, the members of the second swarm fashioned the planets into abodes suited for the beings who would dwell on them, and then kindled the spark of life in the substance of that plane best suited to each planet. Today they each have one body, of the substance of the causal plane, and they are responsible for what we call the laws of chemistry and biology.

5. The swarm that eventually became the Lords of Mind began its pilgrimage after the Lords of Form had completed theirs, when each planet was inhabited by the simple forms of life best suited for it but more complex living things had yet to emerge. We know little about their lives and labors on other worlds, but they arrived on Earth when the only living things were simple single-celled organisms. From these, over the course of ages, they brought complex plants and animals into being, and then kindled the spark of intelligence in those animal forms who were ready to receive it. Today they each have two bodies, made of the substance of the causal and spiritual planes, and they are responsible for what we call the laws of ethology (animal behavior) and psychology.

6. Our swarm, the fourth swarm in this solar system, began its pilgrimage after the Lords of Mind had completed theirs, and the solar system had reached its current state. Our lives and labors, here on Earth and in the other worlds of the solar system, will take the solar system another step closer to the fulfillment of its potentials, and kindle something new in the solar system—the spark of individual self-awareness and free will. When we have completed our pilgrimage down and back up the planes, we too will become an order of spiritual beings in the service of the Solar Logos. In that distant age we will each have three bodies, made of the substance of

the causal, spiritual, and mental planes, and we will be responsible for what we have only dimly and incompletely begun to grasp as the laws of sociology and political science. According to some occult teachings, we will then be called the Lords of Freedom.
7. Though most people are never aware of their presence, the Lords of Flame, Form, and Mind are constantly at work in this and the other worlds of our solar system. Every part of what we call inanimate nature is under the direction of an angel; every species of living thing is under the guidance of a deva; and every religious, spiritual, and occult tradition among human beings has one or more intelligences working with it to help the souls of our swarm pursue the work of spiritual evolution. Thus the help and blessing of greater and wiser beings is always available to us, so long as we are willing to accept their guidance.

Awareness exercise

During the week you spend on this lesson, as you go about your daily activities, think of the presence of the Lords of Flame, Form, and Mind behind everything you experience. When you encounter the forces of nature, think of them as acts of the Lords of Flame; when you encounter living things, think of the Lords of Form guiding them; and when you encounter thinking beings, think of the Lords of Mind helping them to awaken and rise to higher planes of consciousness. See what this does to the way you think and feel about your surroundings.

Affirmation

"I honor the labors of the first three swarms—in the world and in myself."

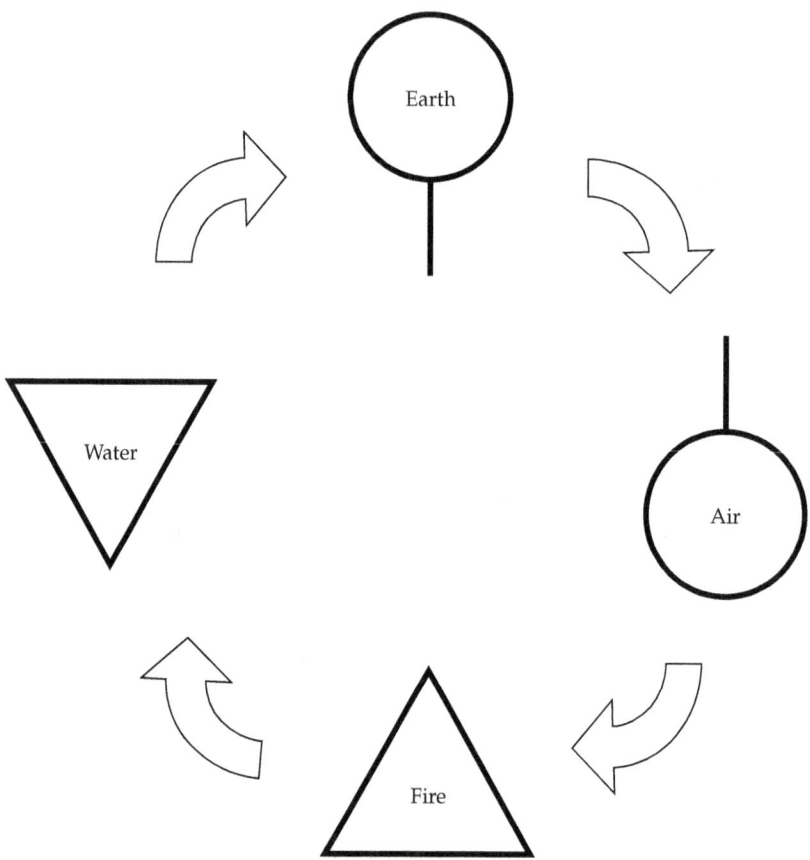

The four elements of occult tradition—earth, water, air, and fire—are each inhabited by beings known as elementals, who were created by the Lords of Flame eartly n the history of the solar system. As creations of the created, elementals have no Divine Spark and they can only evolve spiritually by participating in the evolution of souls such as ours.

LESSON 16

The elementals

1. In the process of bringing the solar system into being, the Lords of Flame, Form, and Mind did not labor alone. Like us and most other created beings, the Lords of the first three swarms have divine sparks at the center of their beings, and received guidance from the Solar Logos through that point of contact with the divine plane. Like us and all other created beings, they were guided and directed in their work by the influence of the twelve Star Logoi. In addition, while the Lords of Form were evolving, they had the guidance and help of the Lords of Flame, and the Lords of Flame and Form both assisted the Lords of Mind in their evolution, just as all three of the primal swarms assist us today.
2. As explained in previous lessons, the Solar Logos and the Star Logoi passed through the process of spiritual evolution countless ages ago, in worlds that have long since passed out of existence, and the Lords of Flame, Form, and Mind passed through that same process in earlier periods of our solar system's history. Our solar system contains another class of beings, however, that do not evolve spiritually in the same way that we do, as the Logoi and the Lords of Flame, Form, and Mind have already done. Among this other class of beings are the elementals.

3. In occult teachings, the elementals are traditionally divided into four broad categories based on the four elements of earth, water, air, and fire. Scientists now have other names for these four kinds of material substance—solids, liquids, gases, and energy—and as you learned in an earlier lesson, they are the four lower sub-planes of the material plane. The elementals of earth are traditionally called "gnomes", those of water are called "undines", those of air are called "sylphs", and those of fire are called "salamanders". (This word originally meant a fire spirit, and came to be used later for a class of small animals related to frogs because these sometimes live in fallen logs, and scurry out of their homes when the logs are put in the fireplace.)

4. Unlike us and most of the other beings in this solar system, the elementals did not come into being through the process of spiritual evolution outlined in Lesson 11. They did not descend through the planes in a subjective state and then rise through the planes again in an objective state, as other beings have done and as we are doing. They were created by the Lords of Flame in the early days of the solar system, when all that existed was chaos and darkness, before the planets were formed and the Sun was kindled. They labored under the direction of the Lords of Flame to build the solar system, and they still work to keep the forces of nature in balance so that souls can evolve on the eight planets.

5. Because they did not originate on the divine plane and do not have divine sparks, the elementals have no inner link to the divine plane and so cannot evolve in the same way as we do. Instead, they evolve by sharing the experiences of the souls who are present on the planet they inhabit. The elementals of this planet—gnomes, undines, sylphs, and salamanders—participate in the lives of all the souls who dwell on Earth, from those in bodies of seemingly inanimate matter through plants, animals, humans, and higher spiritual beings. As we strive and learn, they learn with us.

6. The greatest of the elementals are the planetary spirits, and the planetary spirit of Earth—the great being that many people call Gaia or Mother Nature—is the ruler of all the elementals on and around this planet. Subordinate to her are the four Elemental Kings: Ghob, the king of the gnomes; Nichsa, the king of the undines; Paralda, the king of the sylphs; and Djin, the king of the salamanders. Each of these kings rules an immense number of elementals of many kinds, great and small. Under the direction of the Lords of Flame, they maintain

the balance of elemental forces on Earth and are responsible for all the processes of material nature.

7. Because elementals can evolve through contact with humans, they are often willing to work with us directly. The stonemason who senses unseen flaws in a block of marble, the sailor who can read the waves and winds at a glance, the blacksmith who knows exactly what the fire of the forge will and won't do—these and many others have learned to listen, consciously or not, to the whispered advice of the elementals. Occultists very often cultivate relationships with elementals, using the tools of occult practice to converse with them and ask for their help in matters relating to their element. This brings with it a great responsibility, however, for elementals lack a divine spark and therefore have no conscience, and the consequences of their deeds fall entirely on the occultist who makes use of them.

Awareness exercise

During the week you spend on this lesson, as you go about your daily activities, notice the four lower sub-planes of the material plane around you: solid matter, liquid matter, gaseous matter, and energy. Think of each of them as being shaped and guided by elementals of the appropriate kind. Imagine the elementals going about their lives, maintaining the balance of nature in their elements, always attentive to guidance from the Lords of Flame that created them. Recognize how much of your life depends on the regular working of the material plane, and silently express your gratitude to the elementals for their work.

Affirmation

"I offer my blessing and my thanks—to the elemental beings around me."

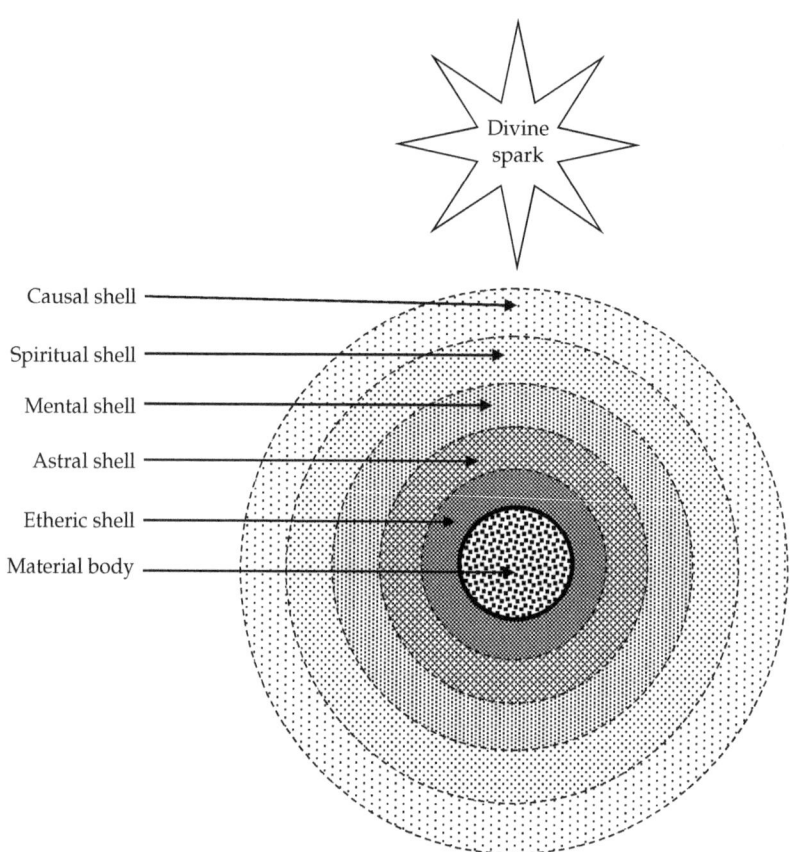

The first stage of evolution into objective form is in the mineral kingdom, the realm of the elements. Here souls evolve material bodies out of the material shell acquired during the subjective or descending arc. The Dvine Spark and all the other parts of the soul remain in subjective consciousness, which is equivalent in some ways to a state of deep trance. Meanwhile the elementals under the guidance of the Lords of Flame help the evolutionary process along.

LESSON 17

The mineral kingdom

1. As you learned back in Lesson 11, each of us began our journey when a divine spark left the divine plane and began its descent through the planes in a subjective state, taking on bodies of the substance of each plane. Having completed the long journey down the planes to the realm of dense matter, we each began to waken to objective existence, beginning with the material plane itself. To understand the process that we as human beings are passing through now, it will be helpful to understand how that process unfolded.
2. For this purpose, imagine a soul that has just completed its descent into matter and is at the very beginning of its evolutionary journey. It exists on all seven of the planes of being; it has a divine spark surrounded by shells made of cosmic root substance in its causal, spiritual, mental, astral, etheric, and material forms; but none of these have yet become a body—that is, an organized, structured, sensitive, and active vehicle composed of the substance of its plane, and capable of experiencing and acting on that plane. Building a body on each plane is the main task of the soul on the ascending arc of its evolution.
3. The first task that confronts the soul on the material plane is thus the task of building a material body. This body is not alive, for life is a

product of the etheric plane. It feels nothing, for feeling is a function of the astral plane. It knows nothing, for knowledge is a function of the mental plane—a function that we as human beings are just beginning to develop. Every capacity of the soul except simple material existence remains subjective. We can think of the soul as sunk deep in trance, dreaming a dim dream of material form.

4. The material body of a soul in this condition is made up of the ordinary substance of the material plane. Since the soul does not yet have an etheric body, or even an etheric sheath, its material body is formed of nonliving matter. A soul at this stage of the process of evolution may be embodied in wind, water, soil, stone, or any other material substance, and souls go through many such embodiments before they complete the process of becoming objective on the material plane. No obvious boundary separates the material body of one soul on this level from the material body of another. That comes with the next stage in the journey.

5. The elementals have an important role to play in this phase of spiritual evolution. They are responsible for sustaining certain regular patterns of change on the material plane—the patterns that scientists call the laws of nature. As souls become objective on the material plane, they are helped by the elementals to attune themselves to those patterns and accept the limits of the laws of nature, so that the souls can use those laws for their own benefit later on. This same principle applies all through the process of spiritual evolution: to accept the limits of a law is to gain the power to use that law.

6. In their work with souls in the mineral kingdom, the elementals are guided by the Lords of Flame, who are the guardians of the laws and forces of nature. It is therefore at this stage of our spiritual evolution that we came closest to the Lords of Flame and received the spiritual imprint of their presence. Their imprint remains even after we have risen from the mineral kingdom through the plant and animal kingdoms to our present condition at the uppermost edge of the animal kingdom. Notice how often simple material substances such as stone, metal, water, air, or fire play important roles in spiritual practice and stir primal reactions in most people. We can sum up this subtle relationship by saying that the Lords of Flame are the guardians and initiators of the mineral kingdom.

7. At the summit of the mineral kingdom are the various kinds of crystals. These are the transitional forms between the mineral and the

plant kingdom. Like everything else in the mineral kingdom, they have a material body, but they also have something else—an etheric sheath, the first tentative form of what will become an etheric body as the souls that inhabit those crystals proceed through the process of evolution. Many people notice that crystals feel "alive" in ways that many other material objects do not. These people can sense the etheric sheath, which is made of life force and will eventually become an etheric body, once the soul of the crystal is reborn as a plant.

Awareness exercise

During the week you spend on this lesson, as you go about your daily activities, notice as you did the previous week the four lower subplanes of the material plane around you: solid matter, liquid matter, gaseous matter, and energy. This time, instead of thinking about the elementals and their work, think about the souls incarnate in the matter and energy that surrounds you, slowly developing the ability to build material bodies, evolving toward the point at which they can pass on to a more complex form of embodiment. Remember that long ages ago you were once in the same condition, just beginning the process of awakening to objective life and consciousness. Greet them silently as your younger brothers and sisters.

Affirmation

"I offer my blessing and my thanks—to the souls of the mineral kingdom."

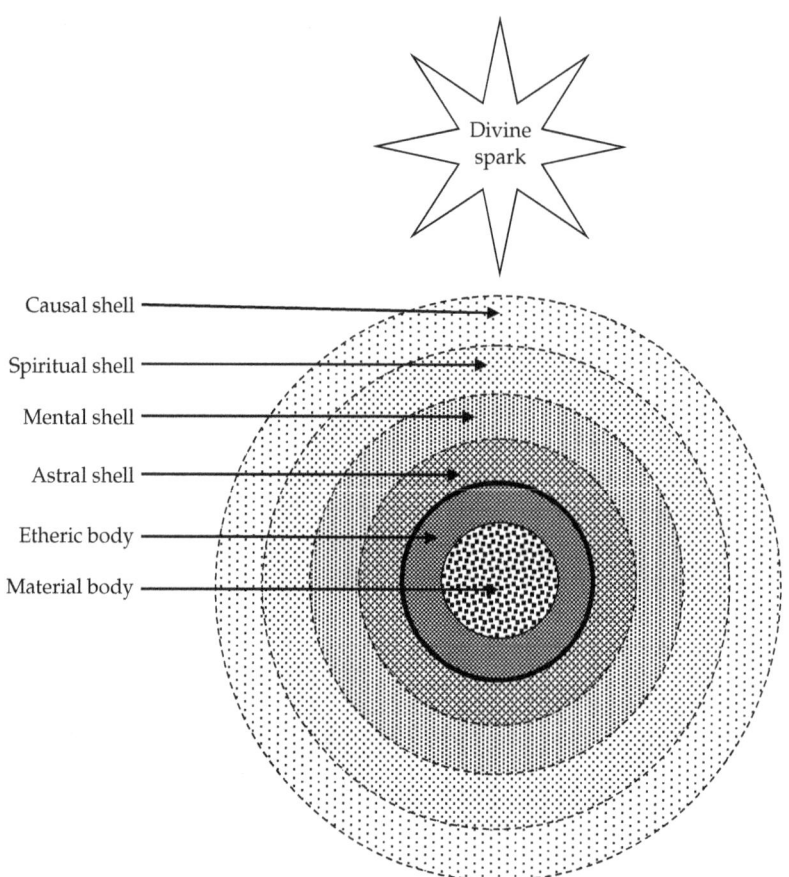

The second stage of evolution takes place in the plant kingdom. Here souls evolve etheric bodies in addition to the material bodies they evolved in the mineral kingdom, using the etheric shell acquired in the descending arc as a basis. All the higher shells remain in a state of subjective consciouosness equivalent in some ways to sleep. While souls are in this state, the Lords of Form and the group-souls of their species guide them toward the next level of being.

LESSON 18

The plant kingdom

1. As souls finish perfecting the ability to form a material body, and start to attain objective existence on the etheric plane, they are reborn into a plant body and begin a series of incarnations in the plant kingdom. Over the course of these incarnations they develop their ability to form an etheric body, finish the process of awakening on the etheric level, and then begin to develop an astral sheath, which brings them to the threshold of the animal kingdom.
2. At this second level of spiritual evolution, the soul can begin to sense the world around it, and it can move in response. A seed sprouting underground can sense the sunlight above, and sends its shoot infallibly up into the light while its root pushes downward into the soil. Many flowering plants turn their blossoms to face the Sun, or open their petals when the Sun shines and close them again when it sinks below the horizon. We can think of the soul as sleeping, and reacting to the things around it in the vague unconscious way that you do when you are asleep.
3. Souls at this stage of their evolution become individualized on the material plane. That is to say, their material bodies become more distinct from the material bodies inhabited by other souls, and from the

world around them. Souls that are incarnated in the mineral kingdom are for all practical purposes identical with each other, and their material bodies mingle freely. No boundary divides the bodies of souls that are incarnate in fire, air, or water. Only when souls enter the element of earth do they become embodied as individual crystals—grains of sand, particles of rock, or the like—and when this happens, they have already evolved an etheric sheath and are preparing to go onward to the plant level.

4. Plants, by contrast, are much more distinct from their material surroundings and from one another. The simplest of plants have cell walls drawing a boundary between their material bodies and everything else on the material plane. Many plants have more robust boundaries—think of tree bark, the leathery surface of holly leaves, or the spines of a cactus. Yet no plant is as distinct from its surroundings as animals are. Rooted in place, blending with soil and air and other living things in complex ways, the plant kingdom is in transition between the unity of the mineral kingdom and the individual identity of the animal kingdom.

5. As the Lords of Flame are the guardians and initiators of the mineral kingdom, the Lords of Form are the guardians and initiators of the plant kingdom. Each species of plants has a Lord of Form who takes charge of the sleeping souls incarnated in that species, and helps them blossom into objective existence on the etheric level. All Lords of Form are especially attuned to the plant kingdom. Notice how often plant products such as bread, wine, and incense are used in sacred rituals and how they stir powerful reactions in human beings. Those reactions are echoes of our interactions with the Lords of Form when we were passing through the plant kingdom long ages ago, and also of humanity's many interactions with them since that time.

6. In the plant kingdom, group souls come into play. A group soul, like an elemental, has no divine spark and no direct connection with the Solar Logos. Group souls are created by the Lords of Form to guide groups of living things, and they evolve through the experiences of the individual souls they guide and direct. Each species has its own group soul, but so do smaller groups of living things. Many people have noticed that certain places have their own distinct personality. In ancient times, people spoke of "dryads" who were the souls of groves of trees, "oreads" who were the souls of mountains,

and so on. These are among the group souls of nature, and they have an especially close connection with the plant kingdom.

7. At the summit of the plant kingdom are the various species of trees. These are the transitional forms between the plant and the animal kingdom. Like everything else in the plant kingdom, they have material and etheric bodies, but they also have something else—an astral sheath, the first tentative form of what will become an astral body as the souls that inhabit those trees proceed through the process of evolution. Many people notice that trees have their own personalities and seem to have their own emotions. These people can sense the astral sheath of the tree, which is akin to the human astral body—the body of emotions and images—and will become an astral body, once the soul of the tree is reborn as an animal.

Awareness exercise

During the week you spend on this lesson, notice the plant life around you. Not all plants are as obvious as trees and flowers! Look for weeds and patches of moss, the faint green coloring on stone and old concrete that tells you that blue-green algae have found a home there. Think about the souls incarnate in plant form all over the world, evolving toward the point at which they can pass on to a more complex form of embodiment. Remember that long ages ago you were once in the same condition, gradually awakening to objective life and consciousness on the plane of the life force. Greet them silently as your younger brothers and sisters.

Affirmation

"I offer my blessing and my thanks—to the souls of the plant kingdom."

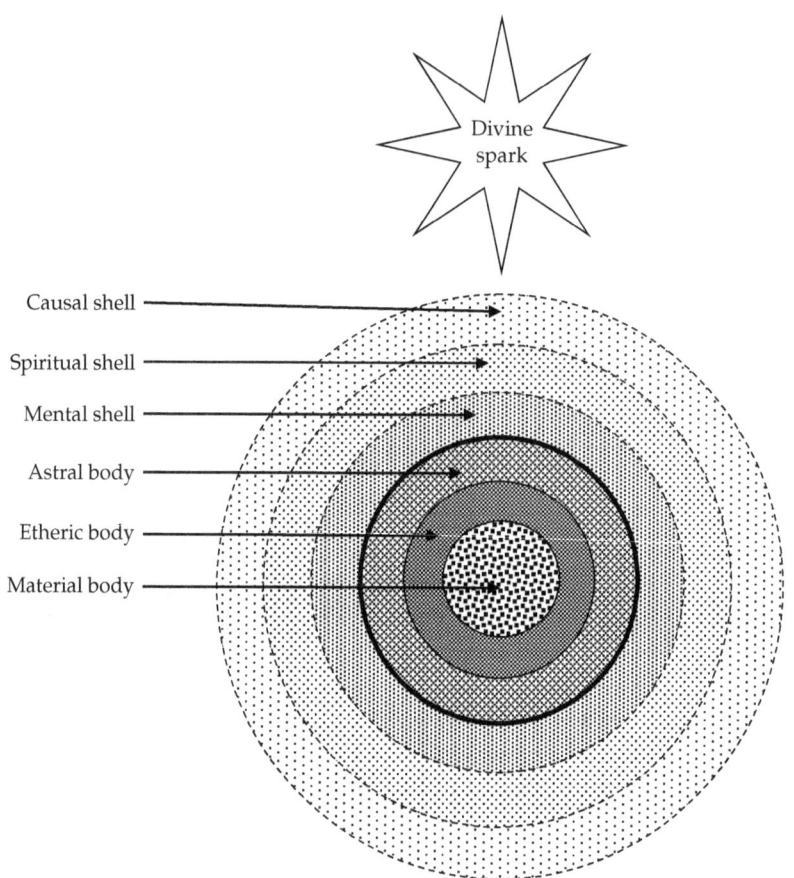

The third stage of the evolutionary process takes place in the animal kingdom. Souls at this stage evolve astral bodies to complement the material and etheric bodies they developed at earlier stages in their evolution. The astral shell acquired in the descending arc provides the raw material for the astral body's construction. The mental, spiritual, and causal shells remain in subjective consciousness, in a state equivalent in some ways to dreaming. During this stage of evolution the Lords of Mind and group souls guide the indvidual souls as they move toward the point at which they must take charge of their own evolution.

LESSON 19

The animal kingdom

1. As souls finish developing the ability to form an etheric body, and start to wake up into objective consciousness on the astral plane, they are reborn into an animal body and begin a series of incarnations in the animal kingdom. Over the course of these incarnations they develop the ability to form an astral body, finish the process of awakening on the astral level, and then begin to develop a mental sheath, the level of the self that separates the animal from the human.
2. At this third level of spiritual evolution, the soul can sense the world around it and respond to it. Souls incarnated as animals have a vivid inner life, full of emotions, memories, and desires; they can recall past events, and hope or fear for the future. These and similar capacities show the presence of objective consciousness on the astral plane. In a certain sense, we can think of the soul at this level as dreaming. When you are dreaming, you have strong feelings, hopes, fears, and other astral experiences, but cannot reason or think clearly. Souls incarnate in the animal kingdom are in the same condition, though they also perceive the world around them.
3. Just as plants are individualized on the material plane, animals are individualized on the material and etheric planes. The life force no

longer streams through them like a river. It forms a stable structure which occultists call the "etheric aura". The etheric aura relates to the rest of the etheric plane in much the same way that the material body relates to the rest of the material plane; both bodies absorb nourishment from their surroundings and expel waste, but both have boundaries that limit what enters and leaves. All animals have an etheric aura extending some distance out from their material bodies.

4. Plants have only a single, sleeping consciousness. Because animals have begun to awaken to the astral plane, they have a twofold consciousness. They have an objective mind, oriented toward the world around them, and they have a subjective mind, oriented to the world within them, the world of feelings and subjective experience. In the simplest animals, these two minds have barely begun to separate. The more complex and intelligent an animal becomes, the more distinct the two minds are. In the most complex animals, such as human beings, the objective and subjective minds are centered in different parts of the body; in us, the objective mind is centered in the brain and the subjective mind in the solar plexus.

5. As the Lords of Flame are the guardians and initiators of the mineral kingdom and the Lords of Form serve the same role for the plant kingdom, the Lords of Mind do this for the animal kingdom. Each species of animal has a Lord of Mind who takes charge of the dreaming souls incarnated in that species, and guides them through the awakening of objective consciousness on the astral level. All Lords of Mind are especially attuned to the animal kingdom, and in ancient times they often appeared to human beings in animal form, giving rise to the traditions of shamanism and totemism. These are echoes of our interactions with the Lords of Mind when we were passing through the less complex stages of the animal kingdom, and also of humanity's many interactions with them since that time.

6. Like plants, most animals are helped by group souls, which are created by the Lords of Form to guide and direct them. Each animal species that has not yet evolved a mental sheath has a group soul, which is responsible for what scientists call "instincts", and smaller groups of animals can also have group souls. Animals can also share in the group soul of a place or an ecosystem. The influence of group souls is all-important in those animals that live entirely by instinct, and decreases as the individual soul gains objective existence on the astral plane.

7. At the summit of the animal kingdom are those species of animals that have begun to develop a mental sheath. These are the transitional forms between the animal kingdom and the next level of spiritual evolution. Human beings are among these transitional forms, but we are not alone at that level. Whales, porpoises, and a few other species are at the same level. Now and then some individual animal of a different species shows unusual intelligence. These are souls that have finished awakening to objective consciousness on the astral level and started to develop a mental sheath. In their next incarnations, they will be reborn in bodies of one of the transitional forms, so that they can finish the work of this plane and go on to the next.

Awareness exercise

During the week you spend on this lesson, as you go about your daily activities, notice the animal life around you, from the little lives crawling and squirming in the soil to the birds in the air, the fish in the seas, and the living creatures on land Think about the souls incarnate in animal form all over the world, slowly developing the ability to build complex astral bodies, evolving toward the point at which they can develop a mental sheath and become what you are now. Remember that not so long ago you were once in the same condition, gradually awakening to objective life and consciousness on the plane of emotions and images. Greet them silently as your younger brothers and sisters.

Affirmation

"I offer my blessing and my thanks—to the souls of the animal kingdom."

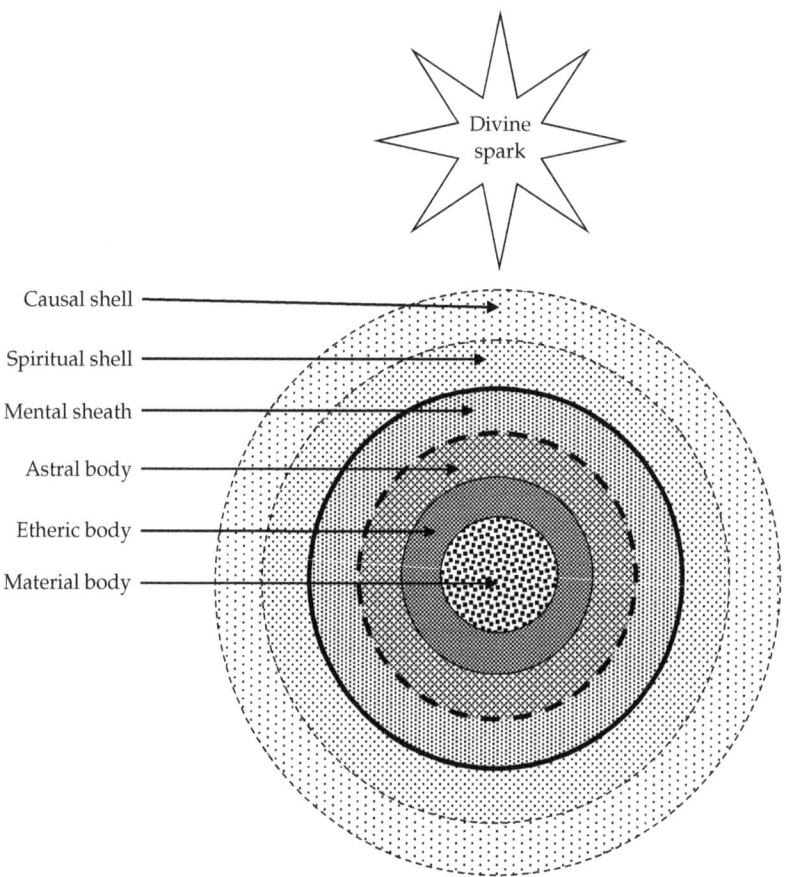

The stage of the evolutionary process we have attained, in the human kingdom, is intermediate between the animal and the spiritual. Souls at this stage have astral, material and etheric bodies and have evolved a mental sheath, the first approximation to a mental body. The mental shell acquired in the descending arc provides the raw material for the mental sheath, and ultimately for a mental body. The spiriutal and causal shells remain in subjective consciousness. During this stage of evolution group souls no longer play a significant role in guiding the individual soul, which must proceed on the evolutionary journey by its own strength.

LESSON 20

The human kingdom

1. The human kingdom, so called, is not really separate from the animal kingdom in the same way that the animal kingdom is separate from the plant kingdom, or the plant kingdom from the mineral kingdom. Humans are animals in most senses that matter. Like other animals, we have material, etheric, and astral bodies, we are individualized on the material and etheric levels, and we have objective and subjective minds. The thing that makes us different from other animals is that we have mental sheaths, the first tentative step toward a mental body.
2. Like other souls at this stage of evolution, you evolved the first rough form of a mental sheath while still in animal form, and in the incarnation after you accomplished that, you were reborn as a human being. Under most circumstances, you will continue to be reborn as a human being until you finish the process of developing your mental sheath into a mental body. Just like the material body, the mental sheath gains strength and definition through exercise, and so the more you work with your mental sheath in each incarnation, the more quickly you will develop it. The more you neglect it, the longer you will drift through human life.

3. The processes by which souls at the human level develop their mental sheaths into mental bodies will be discussed in more detail in the next lesson. For the present, it is important to realize that human beings exist at every possible stage in that process. Some of us have only the most rudimentary mental sheaths and can only just begin to glimpse the lowest expressions of the mental plane. Some of us have developed our mental sheaths to such an extent that they are on the brink of attaining the simplest form of mental body, and a very few of us—the saints and sages among us—have completed the work and will not be reborn again as human beings. The vast majority of us are in between, with mental sheaths of varying levels of development.

4. Occult tradition thus recognizes that different people have different needs in life based on their evolutionary state. A soul who has only just evolved a mental sheath would be wasting time trying to understand occult philosophy, while a soul whose mental sheath is well-developed will be drawn to occult philosophy the way a hungry person is drawn to food. That does not make the first soul inferior to the second. It simply means that each soul has its own work to do and its own lessons to learn as it proceeds through each of its incarnations.

5. As a general rule, souls that have just begun the great adventure of human incarnation focus their attention on the material plane, and this is appropriate. At each new stage of the evolutionary process, the soul reviews the lessons of previous stages, starting from the beginning and proceeding from there. Thus souls at the beginning of their human lives work first on the material plane, then on the etheric plane, and then on the astral plane, before finally reaching upward to the mental plane. Each of these steps up the ladder of existence is more difficult for humans than it is for most other animals.

6. Unlike animal species, the human species has no group soul, and the group souls we interact with—group souls of places, of communities, and of nations, among others—have a much less powerful influence over us than they have over animals. Humans thus have to depend on the guidance of their own minds, along with advice from other human beings and group souls. The Lords of Flame, Form, and Mind are also sources of wise advice, but only those who have evolved their mental sheaths to some degree of complexity can interact with them. The tentative, awkward nature of so much of human

life comes from this. Like children just learning to walk, we totter clumsily through life and trip over our own feet far too often!
7. It is important to accept this, and not to pretend to a stage of spiritual evolution we have not yet reached. As human beings we are in a transitional state. As the old saying has it, we stand halfway between the apes and the angels, and this is the appropriate place for us at this stage in our long pilgrimage through the planes. Furthermore, each of us is at the stage of human existence we have reached by our own efforts in previous incarnations, and our efforts in this incarnation will determine the stage of human existence we will experience in our next lives.

Awareness exercise

During the week you spend on this lesson, as you go about your daily activities, notice which of the planes of existence affects you most. Do you pay attention mostly to the material plane, the realm of matter and energy? To the passions and desires of the etheric plane? To the emotions and images of the astral plane? To the meanings and values of the mental plane? Remember that every human soul spends lives dealing with each of these, and no single stage in that process is better or worse than any other. As you pay attention to how the planes affect you, see if you can get some sense of where you are in your journey through the human kingdom.

Affirmation

"I am a spiritual being—learning the lessons of human incarnation."

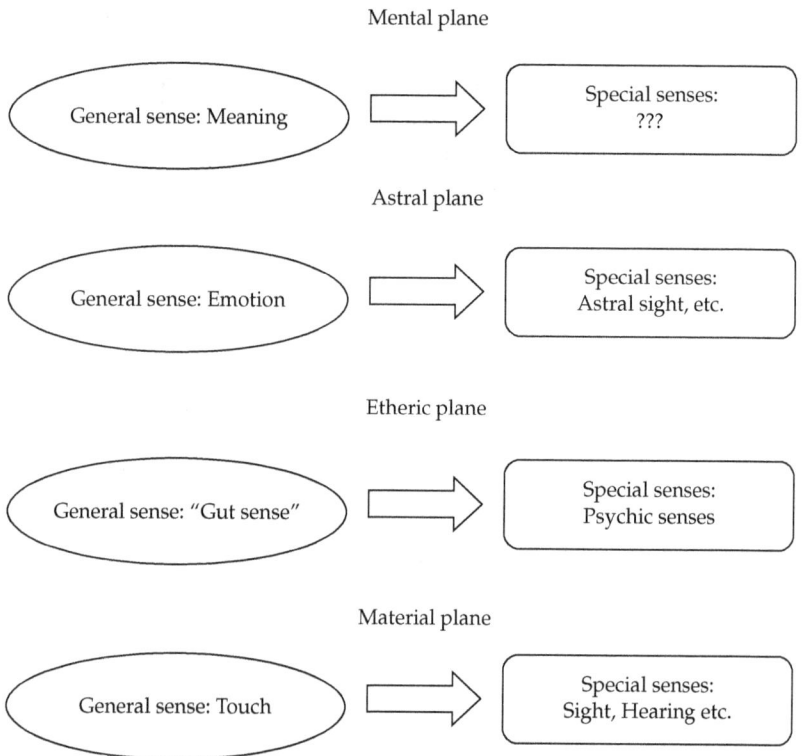

Each body we have already evolved has a general sense and several special senses—for example, the material body has the general sense we call touch, and the specific senses called sight, hearing, smell, and taste. The mental sheath at our current stage of evolution has a general sense, which is the sense of meaning, but it has not yet evolved special senses. When it does so, the resulting transformation will be as dramatic as though we had only experienced the world by touch and suddenly evolved eyes, ears, and other special sense organs.

LESSON 21

The mental sheath

1. The essential task of evolution at the human level, as explained in earlier lessons, is the development of the mental sheath into a mental body. This development is not something that takes place in a single life. Many human lives must pass before the first tentative mental sheath we each evolved in our last animal incarnation is ready to make the great transition to a mental body, and take us on to the next step on our evolutionary journey.
2. To understand the difference between a mental sheath and a mental body, it helps to pay attention to the bodies you already have. Your material body has special senses, such as sight and hearing. It also has a general sense, which we call touch. The same is true of each body. Our etheric bodies have special etheric senses, though most of us have not developed these, and a general etheric sense, which is one of the things people talk about when they say they have a "gut feeling." In the same way, our astral bodies have special astral senses, which you experience when you think, dream, and imagine, and a general astral sense, which you experience when you feel emotions.
3. At every plane of existence, a body has special senses as well as a general sense, while a sheath has the general sense only. When we finish

our journey through the human kingdom and develop our mental sheaths into mental bodies, we will evolve special mental senses which we cannot yet even imagine. As our mental bodies evolve further beyond the human level, those mental senses will become more numerous, richer and more precise. So will our etheric and astral senses, for those bodies will continue to evolve as we proceed up the planes. This is why the material bodies of animals have more powerful senses and richer capacities for action than the material bodies of plants: their material and etheric bodies have continued to evolve as they mastered the lessons of the astral plane.

4. For the time being, all we have to work with is the general sense that our mental sheaths have, which is the sense of meaning. As explained in Lesson 9, meaning is what makes a vocal sound or a squiggle of ink on paper communicate something beyond itself. As we develop our mental sheaths, we become better able to perceive meanings, and to see differences and relationships between one meaning and another. Just as every four-legged animal is "doggie" to a toddler, human beings early in the process of developing their mental sheaths tend to perceive meaning in broad and simple patterns. Later on, as the mental sheath becomes more complex, perceptions become more subtle and nuanced.

5. This is a core reason why it is essential to recognize the difference between human beings at different stages of their spiritual evolution. No stage is better or worse than any other, and all have to be passed through in their proper order. For those souls who have just begun the adventure of human incarnation, and whose attention is focused on the material plane, meaning is best encountered there. In the world of matter, the influence of the mental plane takes the form of physical grace. The perfect form of the athlete's leap or the craftsperson's labors is an encounter with meaning that speeds the development of the mental sheath.

6. Those souls who have passed through that stage, and whose attention is focused instead on the etheric plane, find meaning in the movements of the life force, and these express themselves most clearly in love and family relationships. This is also the stage of human existence where morality plays its primary role, and so it is no accident that so much moral teaching has to do with sexuality and with the emotional bonds that connect family members. As they pass through this stage, human souls find meaning in their interactions with other

people. This is their encounter with meaning, and it, too, speeds the development of the mental sheath.
7. Only when the physical and etheric planes have been linked up with patterns of meaning from the mental plane can the soul turn its attention to the astral plane and begin to find meaning among the images of that level of existence. Here thinking in the usual sense of the word becomes paramount, and the soul begins to confront the slippery nature of the words it used so carelessly in earlier stages. It is only when this stage is well under way that the soul begins to glimpse realms of meaning that cannot be expressed in the words and images of the astral plane, and once this happens the end of human incarnation is in sight.

Awareness exercise

During the week you spend on this lesson, as you go about your daily activities, pay attention to meaning wherever you encounter it. Now and again, stop yourself and ask what a given word or gesture or symbol actually means, and think about it. Notice how many human quarrels and miscommunications happen because two or more people experience different meanings in relation to the same word or phrase. See if you can become a little more precise in the meanings that you use to communicate with others, and to think with in the privacy of your own mind. Pay attention to what happens when you do so.

Affirmation

"A world of meaning surrounds me—and I am becoming more aware of it."

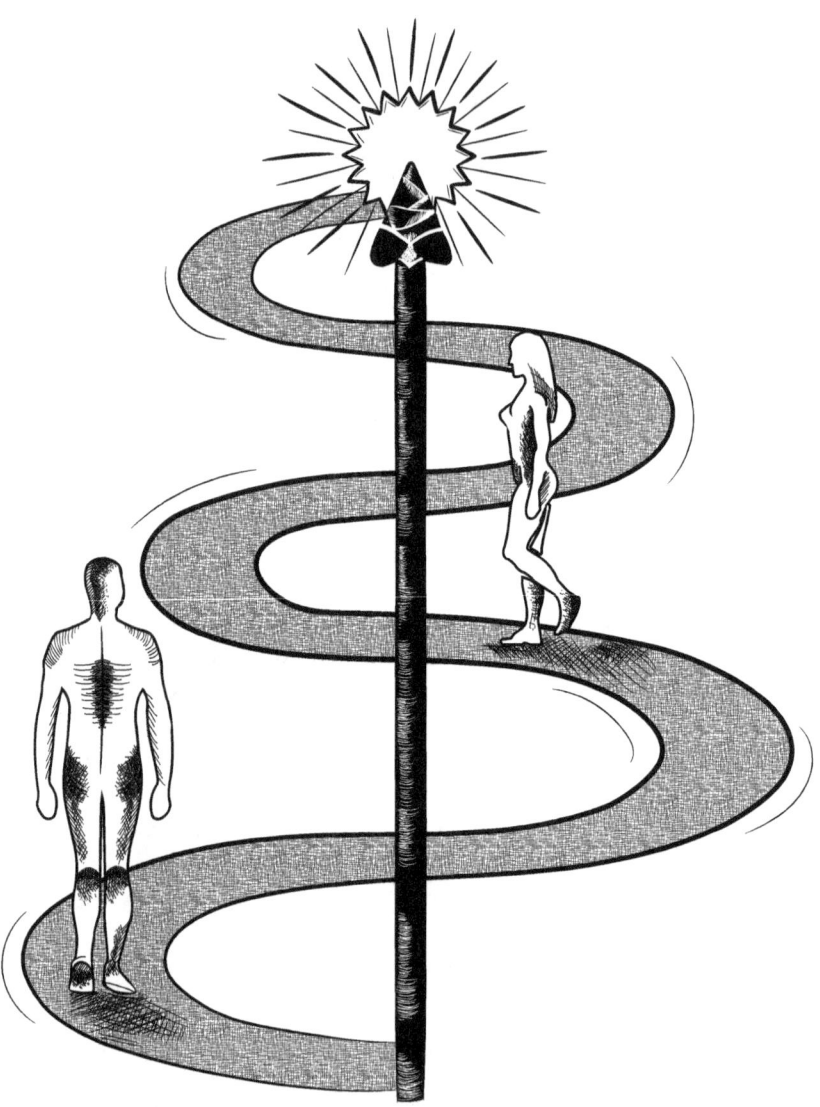

Human spiritual evolution unfolds along two paths. The broad path of everyday life leads eventually to the summit, but it winds from one unbalanced condition to its opposite, and takes many lives to reach its goal. The narrow path of occult study and practice leads straight to the goal and takes far fewer lives. All souls at the human level start out on the broad and winding path, and most remain there, for the narrow path is for the few who feel the call of the great adventure of awakening.

LESSON 22

The two paths

1. The process of human evolution we have discussed in the last two lessons is the ordinary way that most souls take through the transition between the animal kingdom and the realm above human existence. There is another way. The work that takes place through the course of many human lives along the ordinary course of evolution can also be done more quickly through deliberate effort, guided and directed by the knowledge gathered by those who have taken that route before. This is the way of occultism.
2. There is nothing unnatural, in other words, about occult training. It is simply a method of doing in a few lives what the ordinary course of evolution does over many lives. The core techniques of occult practice are methods that have been found to strengthen and develop the mental sheath much more quickly than everyday activities. Occultism also teaches certain other practices that have been found to help keep occult practitioners balanced and healthy while they pursue this work. The teachings of occult philosophy are the ideas and insights that help guide this work to a successful conclusion.
3. The work to be done is the same in essence but individuals and cultures differ, and so no single system of occult training is suited to

everyone. This is why there are many different schools, traditions, and teachings in the realm of occultism. Because each of us has different needs and talents, the basic skills of occult practice have been woven into a variety of techniques and combined in a diversity of ways. If you explore several different systems of occult practice, you will find that one may feel more comfortable to you than another.

4. While methods of occult training differ, certain common patterns exist. First, the individual consciousness must detach itself from the collective consciousness of family, community, nation, and species, so it can think its own thoughts, rather than just repeating the thoughts of others. Once this has been accomplished, the individual consciousness must attune itself with the patterns of the mental plane, first through the reflection of those patterns in the upper subplanes of the astral, and then directly. Just like our muscles, our mental sheath develops with exercise, and the more attention we focus on the mental plane, the more we can experience on that plane.

5. Another way to talk about this process is to say that the goal of occultism is the development of intuition. Intuition is literally in-tuition, inner teaching, the inward knowledge that allows the human mind to grasp what would otherwise be beyond it. When we learn to perceive the reflections of the mental plane in astral words and forms and images, we gain wisdom; when we begin to experience the mental plane more directly, that is called revelation; and when wisdom and revelation become constant conditions of the soul rather than momentary experiences, we have achieved enlightenment.

6. This path is meant for the few. At any given time, roughly a third of the souls incarnate as human beings on our Earth are still in the first stage of evolution discussed in the last lesson, experiencing meaning purely on the material plane. Occultism has nothing to offer them. At any given time, another third of humanity is in the second stage discussed in the last lesson, experiencing meaning through the etheric plane, and occultism has nothing to offer them, either. The remaining third have begun to seek meaning through the astral plane, and much of this work is best done through ordinary learning, study, and creativity. Only those who have come far along the path of exploring the astral plane can benefit from occultism, and not all of them will feel drawn to the occult path; most will continue to follow the way of ordinary evolution instead.

7. Thus there are two paths of human existence, a broad path that most people take and a narrow path that is set apart for the few. There are also two histories of the world, an outer history of peoples and cultures and the rise and fall of civilizations, and an inner history of occult teachings and initiates. Much of that inner history has been secret, since in many ages those who followed the teachings of the inner path have been feared and persecuted by the holders of political and religious power. We can thus speak of an open path and a hidden path, and of an open and hidden history of the world.

Awareness exercise

During the week you spend on this lesson, as you go about your daily activities, pay attention to the way that your occult studies and practices shape your relationships with other people. Notice when, where, and with whom you feel comfortable talking about occultism, and when, where, and with whom it feels wiser to remain silent. Imagine what you would have done if you lived in a time and place where occultism was prohibited and punished by law.

Affirmation

"I follow the inner path of occultism—in the steps of others who have gone before."

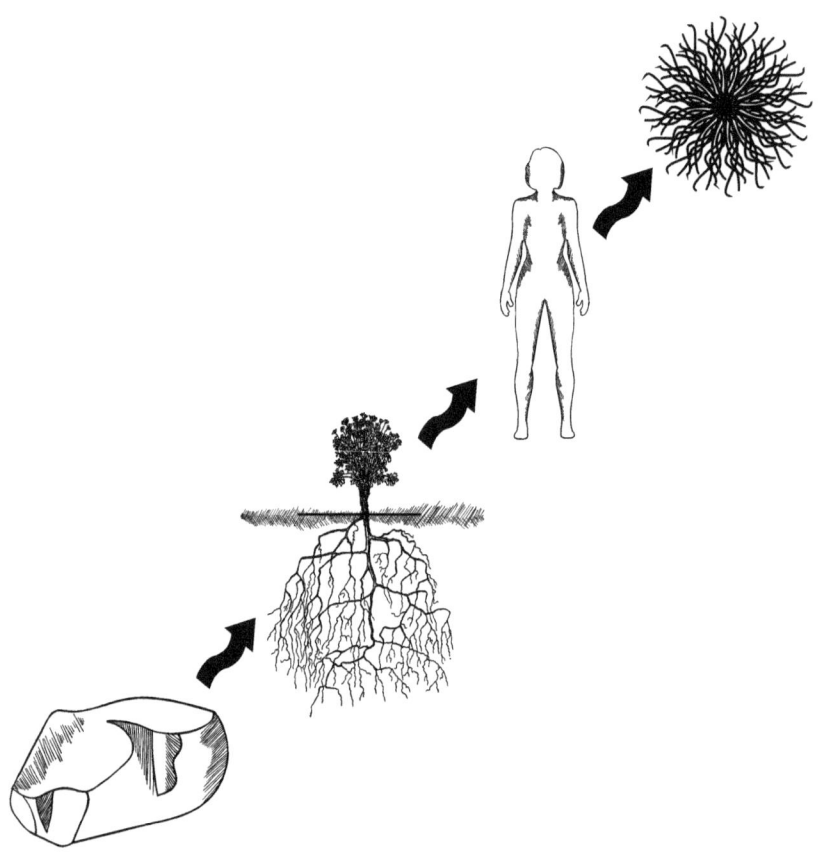

In incarnations long past we have experienced the mineral, plant, and animal kingdoms, and as human beings we are at the highest point of complexity of the animal kingdom, on the brink of the next stage of our evolution. Our work as human beings and initiates is to take that next step and rise above the human level.

LESSON 23

Beyond humanity

1. Both paths described in the previous lesson have the same goal: the evolution of the mental sheath into a mental body. That body, like the material, etheric, and astral bodies, will have its own organs, senses, and capacity to act on its own plane. To have such a body is to make a step in evolution as important as the step from the mineral kingdom to the plant kingdom, or from the plant kingdom to the animal kingdom. It is to enter into an entirely new state of being.
2. When we were incarnate in the mineral kingdom we woke to objective existence on the material plane, and were in a state of consciousness like deep trance. When we were incarnate in the plant kingdom we woke to objective existence on the etheric plane, and were in a state of consciousness like sleep. When we were incarnate in the animal kingdom we woke to objective existence on the astral plane, and were in a state of consciousness like dreaming. As humans we are just beginning to wake to objective existence on the mental plane, and our state of consciousness is like someone on the edge of waking from a dream.
3. By considering these earlier stages through which we have passed, we can learn something about the next stage of our evolution. In that

stage we will wake to objective existence on the mental plane. We will experience meanings not as vague uncertain glimpses but as solid realities, as solid as those of the three planes on which we have already become objective. We will also finish waking up out of the dreaming state of animal consciousness, so that we can think clearly and deeply to an extent that is still beyond us while we are human beings. This much we can know.

4. To a very real extent, however, we can no more understand the state of being we will have at that evolutionary level than a plant could understand what it is to be an animal. That animals are not rooted in place but can move around freely—what a miracle that must look like to a plant! But the greater miracle, the attainment of astral consciousness, goes far beyond that. Even a tree, with its astral sheath and its general astral sense, could not even begin to sense what it would be like to have an astral body, to remember the past and imagine the future, and to have the rich and subtle range of emotions that animals have.

5. So, too, our attempts to imagine the next level of evolution can only reach so far. As we explore our own thoughts and feelings in meditation, we may become aware that human consciousness is still not yet completely awake, and imagine ourselves waking up fully to a world of meaning. The other, special senses that our mental bodies will have are beyond our imagination, and the world of phenomena on the mental plane that we will then begin to experience—that, too, is beyond our imagination at this stage of our existence.

6. The establishment of a mental body, furthermore, is only the beginning of our evolution on the mental plane. Just as plants range from simple single-celled algae on up to mighty California redwoods, and animals range from equally tiny single-celled forms on up to great whales and clever apes, so our embodiment on the mental plane will begin at the simplest level and work up from there to wise and mighty forms we cannot yet conceive of. Long ages will pass before each of us will finish learning how to function on the mental plane, evolve the ability to have richly complex mental bodies, and begin to prepare for the next step in our evolutionary journey, the transition to the spiritual plane.

7. One thing that plants and animals have, however, we will not have once we begin our work on the mental plane: a material body. We are capable of having three bodies at a time. The Lords of Flame never

had bodies at all, for their work was necessary to make it possible for bodies to exist in the first place. The Lords of Form while they were on their evolutionary journey had one body at a time, and their work made it possible for souls to inhabit bodies. The Lords of Mind in their journey had two bodies at a time, and their work made it possible for bodies on two levels to work together. We have three bodies at a time. Only the souls of the seventh and last swarm to pass through evolution in this solar system, unimaginably far in the future, will be able to have all six bodies at the same time, and that will come as the fulfillment of all the labors of all the swarms that came before them.

Awareness exercise

During the week you spend on this lesson, as you go about your daily activities, think about what it would be like to achieve a level of evolution above humanity. Use the description in this lesson as a guide. Even though you cannot imagine it as it will be, the efforts you make to do this will help waken your inner senses and develop your mental sheath.

Affirmation

"I am preparing myself each day—to rise above the human level."

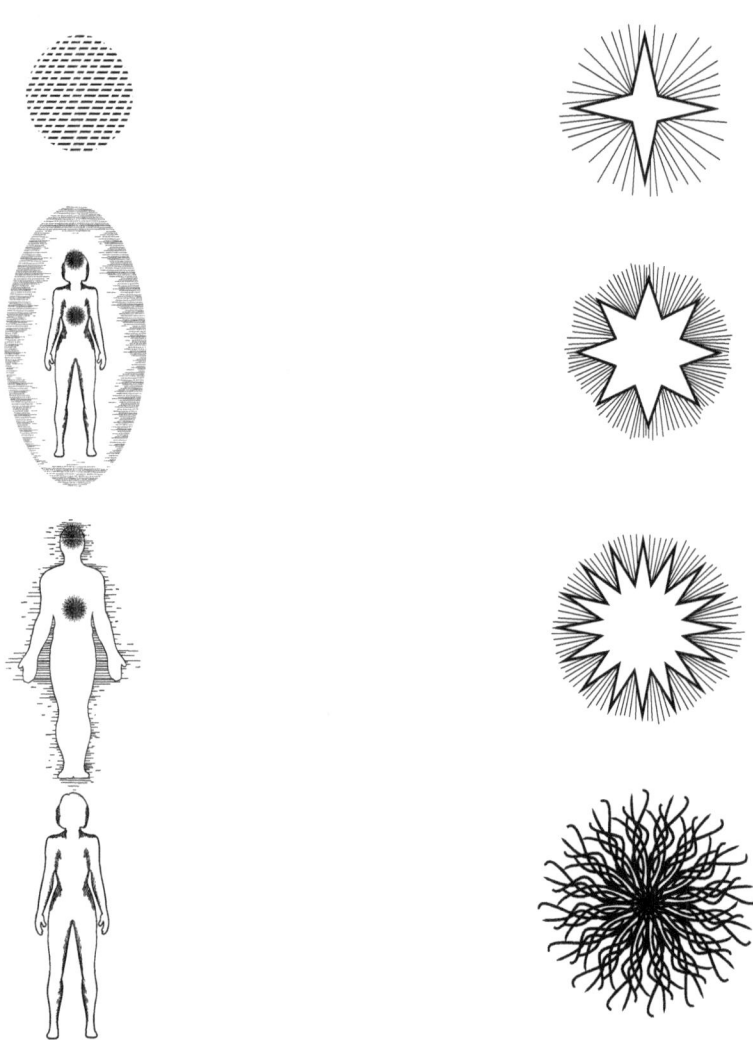

The souls of the fourth swarm, to which we belong, are capable of having three bodies at once. At our present state of evolution we have a material body, an etheric body, and an astral body, surrounding a mental sheath. When we have completed our evolution we will have a mental body, a spiritual body, and a causal body surrounding a Divine Spark.

LESSON 24

The lords of freedom

1. The evolution of a mental body and the awakening to objective existence on the mental plane is therefore far from the end of the evolutionary journey before us. Quite the contrary, it is the halfway point in the ascending arc, three quarters of the way through the whole journey we are making from the divine plane to the material plane and back again. Once we complete the work of building a mental body we will be more than halfway home—but of course that still means that immense ages of further evolution await us.
2. We can only begin to imagine what it will be like to have a mental body and awaken to objective existence on the mental plane, and what we will experience when we become objective on the spiritual, causal, and divine planes is even further from our grasp. All we can do at this stage is reason from what we have experienced on the planes we know. Reasoning along these lines tells us that when we have completed the work that awaits us on the mental plane, we will enter into a transitional state where we will attain a spiritual sheath, transform it by our own efforts to a spiritual body, and shed our etheric bodies.

3. It is important to realize that the shedding of bodies beyond the three that we can maintain will not be a hindrance to us, and will not cut us off from the planes where we no longer have bodies. The Lords of Flame never had bodies at all, and yet they rule the material plane, work with the elementals, and guide the evolution of those beings who are becoming objective on that plane. Similarly, the Lords of Form and Mind no longer have bodies on the planes where we encounter them. Lacking a material body, we will interact with the material plane only when we choose to do so. Since all bodies are made of cosmic root substance, we will not be cut off from the world of matter in any real sense.
4. In the same way, when we have completed our work on the mental plane and evolve a spiritual body, the lack of an etheric body will not hinder us; when we have completed our work on the spiritual plane and evolve a causal body, the lack of an astral body will not hinder us. In our final state of being, with causal, spiritual, and mental bodies surrounding our divine sparks, having passed through all the transformations of the evolutionary process and unfolded all our potentials, we will be able to range up and down the planes at will, as the Lords of Flame, Form, and Mind do now.
5. According to certain occult teachings, as already mentioned, our title in that far future time will be the Lords of Freedom. Where the Lords of Flame are responsible for the laws of the material plane, the Lords of Form for the laws of the etheric plane, and the Lords of Mind for the laws of the astral plane, we will be responsible for the laws of the mental plane. We will guide each of the three swarms that will come after us as they make the transition to the mental plane and pass through their evolution on that plane, and we will help them to become free and self-aware individuals.
6. What makes the transition to the mental plane so challenging for us is that we have no one to do that for us now. We passed through the three lower planes under the guardianship of angels, devas, and intelligences, but as we rise to the mental plane, for the first time in our evolutionary journey, we have to make the transition on our own. The Lords of Flame went through the same challenging experience on the material plane, the Lords of Form on the etheric plane, and the Lords of Mind on the astral plane; the seventh swarm, which will make its evolutionary journey in the far future near the end of

the solar system's long lifespan, will not face it until they rise to the divine plane.
7. What will happen to us and the other six swarms at the end of the solar system's life cycle? Great mystics have reported glimpses of a destiny even more glorious than the one that awaits our swarm within this solar system when we become the Lords of Freedom. The details of that greater destiny remain unknown to us, and at this stage in our evolution, they are probably far beyond our understanding. As children of one of countless solar systems on the seventh cosmic plane of an unimaginably vast cosmos, we have no way of knowing what immense cycles of cosmic evolution await us. In time, however, we will learn.

Awareness exercise

During the week you spend on this lesson, as you go about your daily activities, think about the evolutionary journey discussed in these pages. Try to feel the events of your life as incidents in that great journey, details of the process that is slowly preparing you for your future place in the solar system as one of the Lords of Freedom, a mighty spiritual being tasked with shaping the laws of the mental plane and guiding the swarms of evolving souls who pass through that plane on their own journey. Imagine yourself looking back on this life and its incidents from the perspective of such a being. From that perspective, what does your life today look like?

Affirmation

"I am preparing myself in this life—for my work as a Lord of Freedom."

UNIT THREE

CYCLES OF LIFE AND DEATH

Each of us has lived many times before, in many different bodies and cultures and ages. All these are part of the process by which we experience the potentials and perils of human existence, learn the lessons of this stage of our evolution, and prepare ourselves to go onward.

LESSON 25

The cycle of reincarnation

1. As you have learned in previous lessons, your material body is only one part of the whole structure of yourself, the part that anchors you temporarily in the material plane so that you can learn the lessons of that plane. Dense matter is the most fragile and unstable of all the expressions of cosmic root substance, and so your material body is the most temporary part of you. It is vulnerable to injury and illness, and even if it avoids both of these risks, it will inevitably grow old and die. That reality—the knowledge of our own fragility and mortality—is an essential part of our experience at this stage of our evolution.
2. Since your material body is only one part of you, however, its death is much less important than most people think. Just as you can take off your clothes and walk away from them, you will someday let go of your material body and pass into the unseen. Just as you can put on a different set of clothes, you will someday enter into a new material body and begin a new life on the material plane. This is the cycle of reincarnation, one of the most important teachings of occult philosophy.

3. Spiritual traditions around the world and throughout history have recognized that human existence is not trapped within the bounds of a single life, but passes from life to life, facing new challenges and learning new lessons with each rebirth. Now and again, for various reasons, that insight is obscured, and people become convinced that they have one and only one life, which will be followed either by oblivion or by an unchanging afterlife in a heaven or a hell. Eventually the reality of reincarnation surfaces again, not least because many young children and many practitioners of spiritual disciplines recall bits of their previous lives, and confusion follows as people rethink their beliefs. We are in such a time now.
4. The idea that we only have one life to live has a basis in reality, for the personality formed over the course of a life does not carry over to the next life. The personality, however, is not the soul. The word "personality" comes from the Latin word *persona*, which literally means "mask." The personality is the mask of the soul. One of the benefits of spiritual practices is that they teach you to see past the mask of the personality and perceive your own soul more clearly. When you do this, you come into contact with the part of you that existed long before your present material body was born and will still exist long after that body has died.
5. As we will see, furthermore, beliefs about heavens and hells also have a basis in reality, for the experience of the afterlife differs sharply depending on how the soul spent its life. The differences in question are not a matter of rewards and punishments handed out by Deity, however. They are simply what happens when your soul experiences and processes the thoughts, words, and deeds of your life in the light of objective reality, seeing them as they actually were—not as you want them to be! Another important difference, of course, separates these experiences from the heavens and hells of popular belief: they are temporary, not permanent.
6. Each of the lives you have lived so far as a human being has been part of the process discussed in earlier lessons, the transition that leads from the animal kingdom of objective existence on the astral plane, to the kingdom above humanity, and the attainment of objective existence on the mental plane. The births and deaths, joys and sufferings, loves and hatreds, triumphs and failures you have experienced in your previous lives were all steps in that transition. If this is the first life in which you have taken up occult practice, those lives

were spent on the ordinary path of human evolution; if you took up the work of occult practice in one or more of those lives, some of them belong to the hidden path of occultism. In either case, they are part of the journey that is leading you step by step toward the high destiny of your soul.

7. If you woke up one morning in a tent beside a trail in the wilderness, it would help you a great deal to know where you started the hike, where you had camped the night before, and where you planned on going that day! In the same way, understanding reincarnation makes it much easier to understand where we come from, why we are here, and where we are going. For this reason it has been one of the central teachings of occult philosophy since the most ancient times on record.

Awareness exercise

During the week you spend on this lesson, as you go about your daily activities, try to experience your life as one incarnation out of many. Think about what it might mean if you knew that you have had many lives in the past and will have many lives in the future. See what difference this makes to your attitudes and actions.

Affirmation

> "I existed long before this body was born—and I will exist long after this body dies."

The Soul:

Immortal

Your real self

A center of consciousness

The Personality:

Mortal

Your temporary self

A collection of habits

The relation between your soul and your personality is essential in occult philosophy. Your personality is the temporary vehicle of your consciousness in this life; your soul is the enduring vehicle of your consciousness in countless lives, past and to come. The experienced occultist is able to bring soul and personality into balance, making the personality a flexible and effective expression of the soul.

LESSON 26

The soul and the personality

1. In order to make sense of the process of reincarnation, it is helpful to learn more about the difference between the two selves you have, the soul and the personality. The most important thing to realize is that your soul is your real self. It is who you truly are. It existed long before your current body was born and will still exist long after your current body is dead. While you are incarnate in a material body, however, your soul is in a state much like sleep. The life you are living right now is the dream that your soul is dreaming as it sleeps.
2. Your personality is the image of yourself that your soul has created in its dream. Your personality is not your soul. If you examine your personality closely you will find that it is simply a collection of habits of thinking, feeling, and acting in relation to the world that you experience. It is like a mask that fits over your soul, and as mentioned in the previous lesson, the word "personality" comes from an old Latin word for "mask." In Roman plays, the characters wore masks on stage, to help them represent the parts they were playing. You can think of your personality as the mask you put on when you were born, so you could play your part in the drama of your present life.

3. While it is not your real self, your personality is important, because it is through your personality that your soul can explore different ways of experiencing the human stage of existence. If your personality remained the same through all your incarnations, you would be stuck with one set of habits of thinking, feeling, and acting. Since your soul puts on a new personality with each incarnation, it can select the best parts of each personality to keep, and let go of the parts that didn't work well. Each of the personalities you had in your previous lives helped your soul assemble a set of habits of thinking, feeling, and acting that allows it to express itself as fully as possible on the three planes where it currently has bodies. Your present personality is the latest creation of your soul, and combines habits that have proved to work in previous lives with new habits your soul is trying out.

4. Your personality exists on the astral plane, which as you already know is the plane of ordinary thoughts and feelings. It is one of the aspects of your astral body. Your soul began to create personalities as soon as it evolved an astral body—that is, as soon as it finished its incarnations as a plant and started its incarnations as an animal. If you have spent much time around animals, you probably noticed that they have personalities of their own, sometimes very strong personalities. This is why your soul did not need to learn how to create a personality when it reached its first human life. It had plenty of practice doing that in its animal incarnations.

5. The raw material for your personality comes partly from your soul, and partly from the people you know and the experiences you have during childhood. When you first started having incarnations as a human being, nearly everything in your personality was taken from the people you met and the events that happened to you, but the more human lives you live and the more complex your mental sheath becomes, the more of your personality comes from your soul instead, and reflects the unique qualities of your soul rather than the people and surroundings that shaped your childhood in that incarnation. As a result, over the course of your human incarnations, your personalities become more and more like your soul.

6. Many souls, as they reach the end of their human incarnations, begin to remember scraps of their previous lives. When this happens naturally, it is a sign that you have begun to wake up out of the dream of incarnate existence. As memories of previous lives surface and the

personality integrates them, the personality gradually merges with the soul. More precisely, you realize that you have always been your soul, and your personality is simply one set of habits you took on in a certain incarnation.

7. You have probably had the experience, at some point in your life, of waking up out of a vivid dream. As you finished waking up and found yourself in your bed, instead of wherever the dream had taken you, you may have thought, "Oh! That was just a dream, after all." That experience echoes the one you will have at the end of your human incarnations, when you will wake up out of life in a material body and think, "Oh! That was just a dream, after all."

Awareness exercise

During the week you spend on this lesson, as you go about your daily activities, pay attention to your personality, and see if you can experience it as a collection of habits of thinking, feeling, and acting, rather than as your real self. Notice whether all those habits are useful to you. Do you remember why you took up those habits? Are there good reasons why you might wish to let go of some of them?

Affirmation

"My soul is my true undying self—my personality is the mask that it wears."

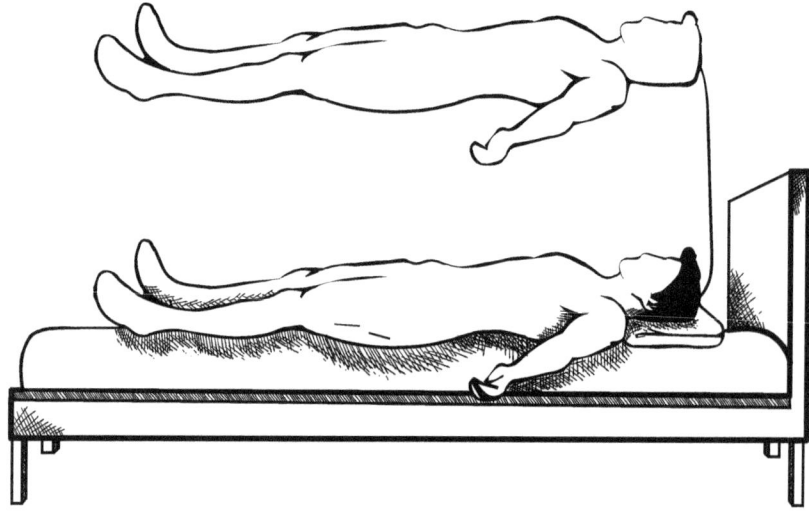

During the first stages of the dying process, before the First Death has taken place, the subtle bodies often drift out of the material body and can be seen by clairvoyants hovering above it, connected by a link that appears to subtle vision as a silver cord. The First Death takes place when the silver cord breaks and the subtle bodies separate permanently from the material body.

LESSON 27

The first death

1. Understanding the nature of life and death is an important part of occult training, for at least two reasons. To begin with, as we have seen, the fear of death is based on the misunderstanding that each of us has only one life. That fear is a great burden to many people, and prevents them from living their lives to the fullest. Learning that death is a transition rather than an end, no more to be feared than going to sleep between one day and the next, is one effective cure for that burden, and leads to a happier, more successful, and more fulfilling life.
2. There is also a practical dimension to knowing the secrets of death. Each of us will die sooner or later, and when we die, knowing what to expect and how to cope with the changes that follow death makes it easier to pass through the process without difficulty or distress. If you knew that someday you would have to travel to a distant place in a country where you have never been, you would want to find out in advance the details of how you would get there and what you would have to do on the way. For exactly the same reason, it is worth finding out about the journey of death before you have to make it.

3. One of the first things to understand about death is that it takes place in several stages, because all of your bodies do not die at once. The material body is the first body to be cast off in the dying process, and occult philosophy therefore refers to the death of the material body as "the first death". The etheric and astral bodies die later, and they each have their own processes to go through, just as the material body does. The mental sheath does not die. When you complete your evolutionary journey and become one of the Lords of Freedom, you will have causal, spiritual, and mental bodies. Your mental body, once you evolve it, will therefore be the first of your permanent bodies. It is the body that will lift you above the cycle of life and death.

4. People die in many different ways, and the nature of the death can have some influence over the soul's experience in the afterlife. When death comes from old age or a prolonged illness, the soul and its higher bodies will usually begin to separate from the material body long before the actual moment of death. Dying people very often spend much of their time sleeping, and this is good for them, because their soul is getting used to existence outside of the physical body and will be able to make the transition more easily. People who have developed the gift of clairvoyance, which allows them to perceive the etheric and astral planes directly, often see the etheric doubles of dying people drifting out of their material bodies and floating a few feet above the material body.

5. When death comes suddenly from accident or injury, the soul has no chance to prepare for the transition, and many souls in this condition end up disoriented for a while after the first death. The same thing can happen when the dying person is terrified of death or of what will happen afterwards—for example, those who are afraid that that they will go to Hell when they die often have a difficult transition, and come through the first death frightened and confused. This makes the early stages of the afterlife much more difficult than they have to be.

6. This is one of the reasons why prayers and ceremonies for the dead are so important. Thoughts and feelings belong to the astral plane, as you have learned, and the prayers of living people can thus have a positive effect on astral conditions. Ceremonies performed by trained clergy or occultists can have an even stronger beneficial effect. Prayers and ceremonies for the dead comfort souls that have just passed through the first death, help them get used to their

new condition, and prepare them for the further stages of the dying process.
7. Another thing that can help a soul pass through the first death without unnecessary difficulty is the practice of imagining one's own death in advance. Since death is a transition rather than an end, this need not be frightening or depressing. Simply imagine yourself as you will be when you are very old, and your material body—the most fragile and unstable of your bodies—is worn out by a long life. Imagine it quietly shutting down, the heart stopping and the last breath slipping out of the lungs. Then imagine yourself rising up out of your material body and turning to look at it. You are still yourself; your soul is clothed in its etheric and astral bodies and its mental sheath, and you can feel your etheric body the way you now feel your material body. This is the first death, the beginning of your journey to a new life.

Awareness exercise

Several times during the week you spend on this lesson, take a few minutes to imagine your own death, as described in paragraph 7, above. Picture it as clearly as you can. Notice what emotions and ideas the process awakens in you. If you feel drawn to do so, read books or websites about near-death experiences (NDEs) to prepare for next week's lesson.

Affirmation

"I have died many times—and been reborn many times."

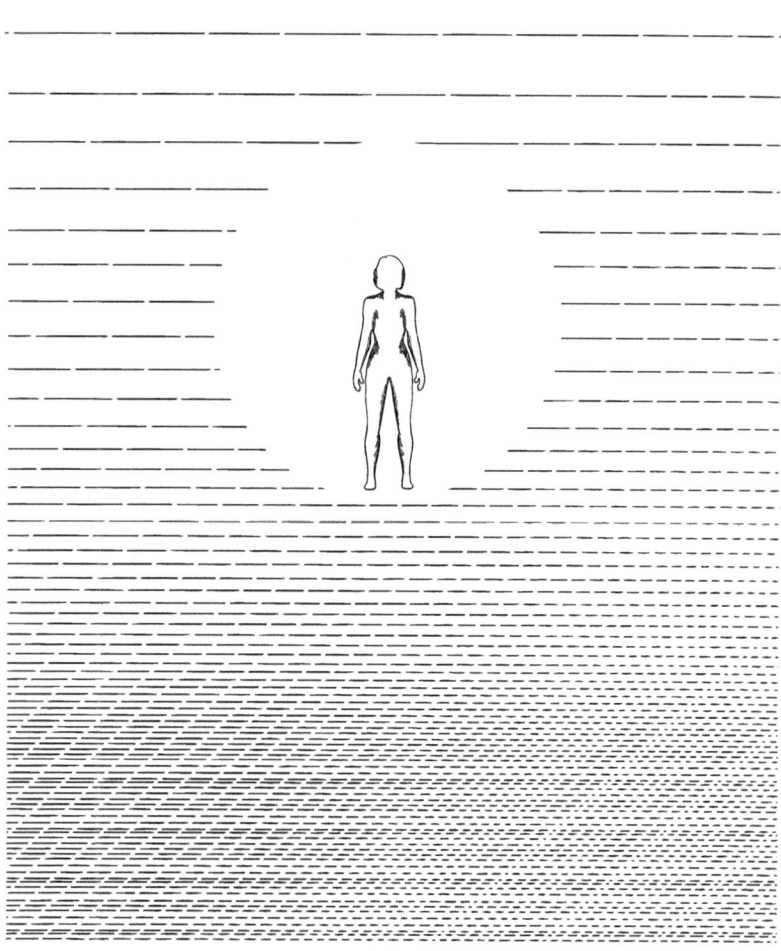

The transition of consciousness from the material plane to the astral plane, one of the phases of the Second Death, is experienced by those who are conscious at the time as rising out of darkness through a tunnel into light. People who have near-death experiences often report this. Most people, however, pass through the Second Death in a state of unconsciousness and simply wake up on the astral plane.

LESSON 28

The second death

1. At the end of the first death the soul and its subtle bodies have separated from the material body. Modern medical technology sometimes allows this to be reversed, if the material body is not too badly damaged. The term "near-death experience" is used by modern researchers to describe the reports of people who have been revived after passing temporarily through the first death. The accounts of people who have had near-death experiences match up exactly with descriptions of the dying process in occult philosophy, and provide an additional source of information on the processes of death and rebirth.
2. Revival after this kind of temporary death is possible because the soul still possesses an etheric body. The etheric plane is the plane of life, and so long as the soul still has a body on the etheric plane it can return to its material body and revive it—again, provided that the material body is still able to function. Once the etheric body dies, however, this is no longer possible. In occult philosophy, the death of the etheric body is called "the second death", and it marks the point at which the dying process becomes irreversible.

3. How much time passes between the first and second deaths depends on a variety of factors, but the most important is the health and strength of the etheric body. A person who is very old at death, or who dies after a long illness, has a weak and fragile etheric body, and in such cases the second death can occur within a few hours, or in some cases within minutes. With a person who is young and in good health, and therefore has a strong and vital etheric body, it can take several days before the second death takes place. The stronger the etheric body, the longer the delay between the first and second deaths.
4. Before the development of modern medical technology, revival after the first death was less common, but it did happen. The most famous example, Jesus of Nazareth, returned to life three days after he passed through the first death; since he was in his early thirties, in good health, and had a carpenter's strong body, this comes as no surprise to occultists. It is very rare for revival from death to happen much later than this, however, because the cellular life of the body usually shuts down after a few days.
5. Most souls that retain consciousness during the first death will experience the same things that have been reported over and over again from near-death experiences. First, after the separation from the material body, the soul finds that it can look down on the material body to see medical personnel gathered around it, or whatever the deathbed scene happens to be. Then, after a short time, the soul's perceptions shift from the material plane to the astral plane—a shift that is often perceived as rising upward through a dark place or tunnel into light. Once the soul becomes aware of the astral plane, it can interact with other beings on that plane, which include souls of other people that have died and not yet been reborn, as well as beings outside of incarnation such as the Lords of Flame, Form, and Mind.
6. Not everyone who passes through the first death will experience these things, however. Many people sink into a state of unconsciousness when they are close to the first death, and remain unconscious until after they pass through the second death. The first phase of the afterlife that such a person experiences is waking up to consciousness of the astral plane, as explained in the next lesson. This is the normal way to pass through these stages of the dying process, and it avoids the risk of becoming temporarily trapped between the first and second deaths, which is rare but happens from time to time.

7. Those souls that have purified and strengthened their subtle bodies through religious, spiritual, or occult practices, however, normally experience the dying process without losing consciousness at any point. Since they have prepared themselves in life, they have nothing to fear from death, and can expect to pass through the first and second deaths easily and without difficulty. Those who have succeeded in developing their mental sheaths into mental bodies always experience the end of their final material incarnation in this way, and many of those who are well on their way to this point do the same.

Awareness exercise

During the week you spend on this lesson, continue the practice of imagining your own death, but take it further. See yourself, after you have observed your material body from outside, rising up through a dark tunnel into the brilliant light and color of the astral plane, where you are greeted by others who are no longer incarnate in material bodies. If you feel drawn to do so, continue to read books or websites about near-death experiences (NDEs).

Affirmation

> "I am making good use of this life—I am prepared for my next death."

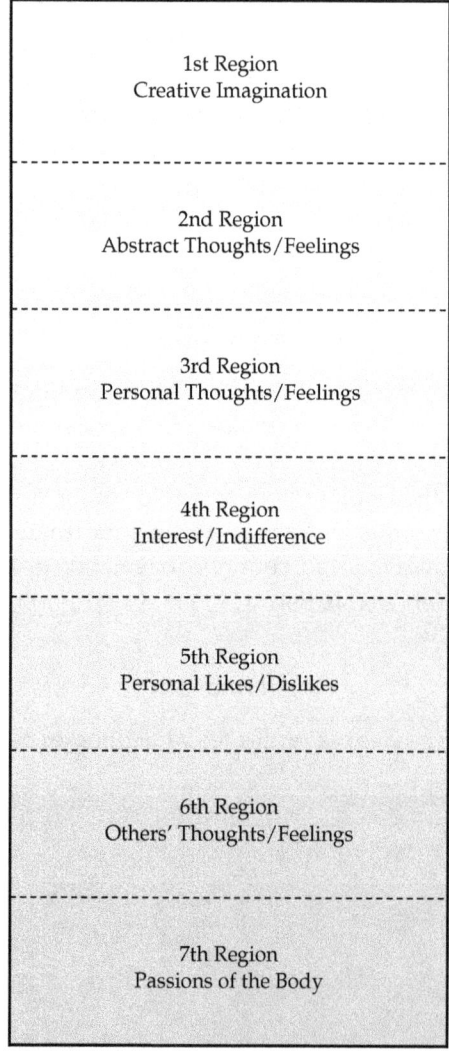

After the Second Death the soul abides in the astral plane and processes the experiences of the life that has just ended. The focus of attention during life determines which region of the astral plane the soul experiences. Depending on the nature of those experiences, this can be heaven—or it can be hell. This has nothing to do with reward or punishment—it is simpoly a function of cause and effect.

LESSON 29

Heaven and hell

1. Once the soul has passed through the first and second deaths, shedding its material and etheric bodies, it is ready to embark on the work that awaits it in the afterlife. Most of this work is done on the astral plane, the plane of thinking, emotions, memories, and imagination. It is here that the soul reviews and absorbs all of its experiences from the life that has just finished. While it does this, it sheds its astral body a portion at a time, so that it can either prepare for another life in a new set of bodies, or begin a new phase of existence at the level of spiritual evolution above incarnate humanity.
2. The process of reviewing and absorbing experiences is sometimes pleasant and sometimes the opposite, depending on the nature of the experiences the soul has had during its most recent life. These experiences, like dreams, correspond to the different regions of the astral plane. After death you will spend most time on the sub-plane that corresponds to the kind of experience that occupied most of your attention in life. If you were mostly interested in pursuing physical passions, for example, you will spend most of your afterlife in the lowest region of the astral plane, while you process the experiences appropriate to that region.

3. In the same way, if you spent most of your life simply following the promptings of ideas and opinions you picked up from other people, you will spend most of your afterlife in the second astral region, and if your own personal likes and dislikes have been your chief concern during your life, you will spend most of your afterlife in the third astral region. These regions, as you have learned, resemble substance, and the dreams that take place in them tend to be darker, more confused, more compulsive, and more frightening than other dreams. The experiences souls have in these regions in the afterlife can be described in similar terms.
4. To the fourth astral region belong interest and indifference, and if what concerned you most in your most recent life was curiosity and the ordinary life of the mind, your soul will spend most of its afterlife in the fourth astral region. Souls spend most of their afterlives in the fifth, sixth, or seventh astral regions if the things that mattered most to them in the life just ended were self-knowledge, wisdom, and the pursuit of creativity and spirituality. Dreams that take place in these higher regions of the astral plane are brighter, clearer, more lucid, and more joyous than other dreams, and the experiences of souls in these regions of the astral plane after death can be described in the same terms.
5. The experiences of souls in the different regions of the astral plane after death are what lies behind popular beliefs about heaven and hell. The three lower regions of the astral plane can be described as the regions of blind passion, ignorance, and selfishness; personalities that are motivated by these three factors very often behave in unethical ways, and the souls that had these personalities will process the resulting experiences in the dark and frightening setting of the lower astral regions. The four higher regions of the astral plane can be described as the regions of thought, self-knowledge, wisdom, and spirituality; personalities that are motivated by these three factors behave in ethical ways, and the souls who had these personalities will process the resulting experiences in the luminous and joyous setting of the upper astral regions.
6. It is important to realize, however, that none of this is a matter of punishment or reward. If you review your own behavior at the end of a busy day and realize that you have made a serious mistake, one that will cost you something you value, the sense of failure and foreboding you feel is unpleasant. If you do the same thing and realize

that you have succeeded at a difficult task and will benefit from it in the future, the sense of relief and accomplishment you feel is pleasant. Your experiences in the afterlife are much the same, though on a much larger scale and with more serious stakes. With the eyes of your soul, unhindered by the limits of your present personality, you will review every thought, word, and action of your life, the good, the bad, and the ugly, accept it all, and learn from it all.

7. One other important difference, of course, distinguishes the experience of the soul on the astral plane from the heaven and hell of popular belief—the sojourn of the soul on the astral plane does not last for all eternity. How much time is required varies depending on the length and intensity of the life that has just been lived, and on the number of astral regions involved, for souls begin at the lowest astral region, process any experiences relevant to that region, and then move up to the next. A soul that has just reached the human level and focused entirely on physical cravings and passions will be finished much sooner than a soul that has had a long and complex life and experienced most or all of the astral regions. One way or another, however, the soul will eventually finish its work on the astral plane and will rise to the mental plane.

Awareness exercise

During the week you spend on this lesson, once a day, spend a few minutes thinking back to some earlier time in your life. Try to remember as much as you can about that time, the good parts and the bad, the successes and the failures. Don't pass judgment on yourself; simply remember. As you do this, be aware that this is a very simple equivalent of what your soul will do when it awakens on the astral plane after this life.

Affirmation

"All that I do in this life—I will remember and process between lives."

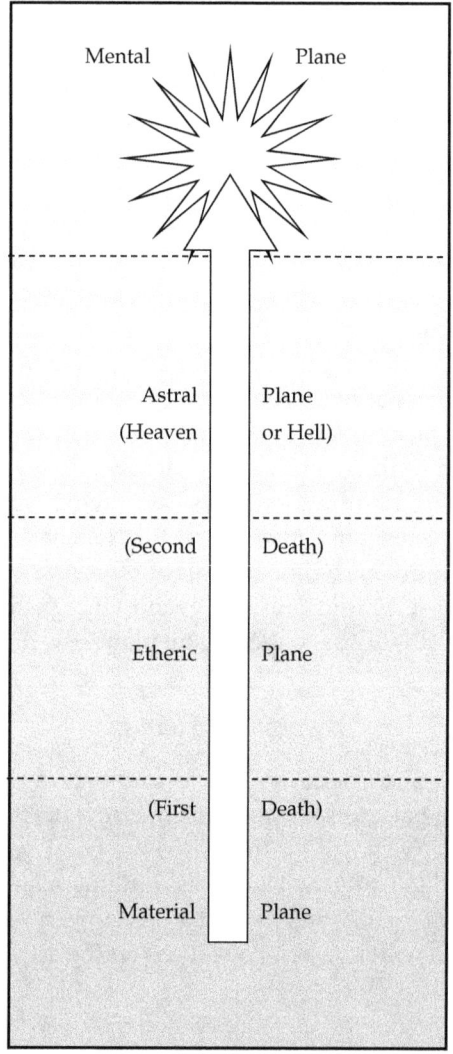

The soul completes its ascent through the planes at the end of each human life with a glimpse of the mental plane, from which it gathers its first concepts of meaning, purpose, and value. As one human life gives way to another, and the mental sheath develops. these glimpses become longer and more detailed, until eventually the soul evolves a mental body and is ready to function on the mental plane.

LESSON 30

The vision of the ideal

1. When the soul finishes its work on the astral plane, it leaves that plane and becomes aware of itself on the mental plane. In the previous stage of the dying process, it has shed its astral body, and its only remaining embodiment is the mental sheath, the seed from which its first permanent body is taking shape. At this point in the afterlife it has risen as far on the planes as it is able, for a soul can enter into objective existence on any plane only if it has a body or a sheath of the substance of that plane.
2. The development of the mental sheath determines how long the soul can remain on the mental plane and how much it can perceive once it is there. For those souls that have just reached the human level and have only rudimentary mental sheaths, the experience of the mental plane is little more than a brief flash of illumination, followed promptly by a new descent through the planes into incarnation. For those souls that have developed their mental sheaths to some extent, the experience is more prolonged and more detailed, while for those who have succeeded in evolving their mental sheaths into mental bodies, the doors of the mental plane open wide and do not close again.

3. As brief and indefinite as it often is, the ascent to the mental plane between lives plays an important role in the life to come. The mental plane is the plane of meaning, and it is the source of our sense of meaning, purpose, and value. When people ask themselves, "What is the meaning of life? What is the purpose behind it all? What value does my life have?" they are reaching back, whether they know it or not, toward their memories of their most recent glimpse of the mental plane, the only plane humans can yet experience where questions of this kind can be answered.
4. It is possible to renew that glimpse of the mental plane while incarnate, and this is one of the goals of meditation and other forms of spiritual practice. Through the disciplines of occult training, it becomes possible to focus the attention on the uppermost regions of the astral plane and to pass above them into the lowest regions of the mental plane. The resulting glimpse of the mental plane is the experience that many people call "enlightenment." One of the most common features of that experience is a sense of homecoming, and that sense is accurate, due to the soul's repeated experience of the mental plane between its incarnations.
5. Because the soul experiences the mental plane only briefly at first, the role of meaning in its first human lives is relatively modest. Since a soul that has just become human has the lessons of the human kingdom to learn before it begins preparing to pass beyond that kingdom, this is appropriate, and most souls spend many lives pursuing the goals set before them by biological passions, social expectations, personal likes and dislikes, or ordinary curiosity: the concerns of the four lowest regions of the astral plane. Only when the soul has passed through these stages and begun to develop its mental sheath will its glimpses of meaning on the mental plane between lives begin to influence its incarnations to any great extent.
6. The afterlife that follows the first serious development of the mental sheath is very often an important turning point for the soul. Very often the soul enters into its next incarnation following this experience with a clear sense of some ideal, which it then pursues throughout the following life. Since it is based on a single glimpse of the mental plane, that ideal may not be clearly understood, and it may be unbalanced or even harmful, but the personality taken on by the soul in that incarnation will pursue it at all costs. From this single glimpse comes those lives that are devoted to a single purpose for good or

ill. When the soul next rises to the mental plane between lives, it will perceive some different facet of the mental plane, and begin to move toward greater balance.

7. The soul that has had repeated glimpses of the mental plane between lives has a more balanced perspective, and knows that the meaning of life is not to be found in a single obsessive purpose. As the mental sheath evolves toward its fulfillment as a mental body, it begins to perceive the mental plane not as a dazzling brilliance but as a landscape of meanings as rich, complex, and varied as the material plane. When this happens, it indicates that the mental sheath has begun to develop its own sense organs, and when that happens liberation from the wheel of life and death is rarely far away.

Awareness exercise

During the week you spend on this lesson, pay attention to what things in your life have meaning and value for you, and think about why you find them meaningful and valuable. Notice especially those things that have meaning and value for you but not for most of the other people you know. When did you first realize that these things are important to you? Why do they matter to you? It is by exploring questions such as these that you can begin to glimpse the influence of your soul's encounters with meaning between lives.

Affirmation

"I have looked on realms of light and meaning—and I will behold them again."

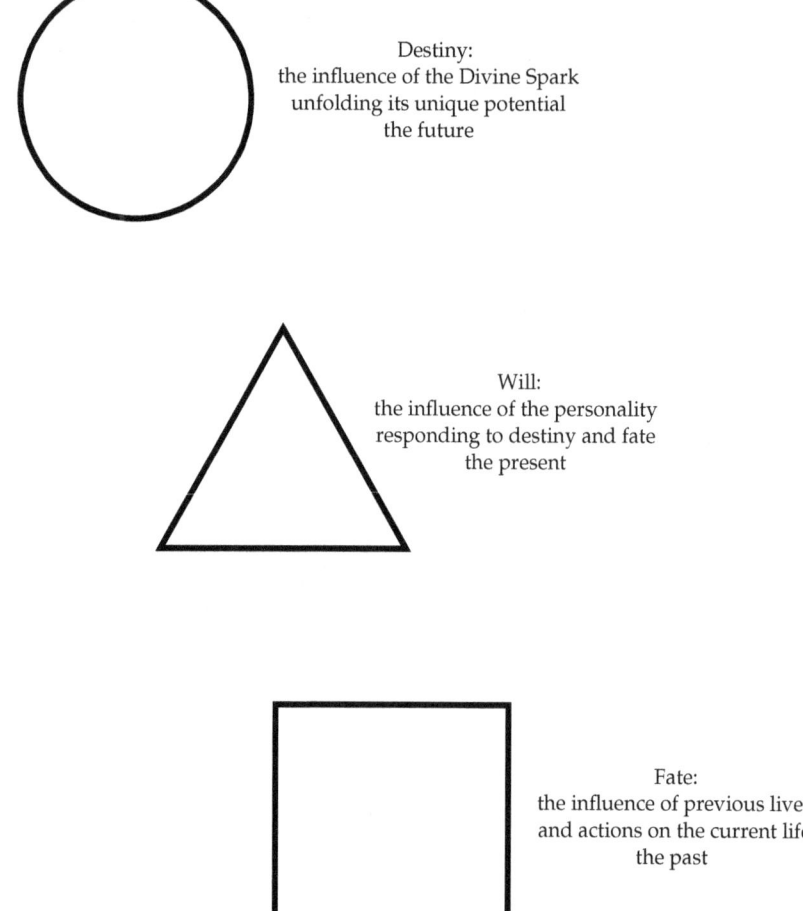

Fate, will, and destiny are the three forces that shape each incarnation. Destiny is the soul's glimpse of its own potentials, while fate is the sum total of the consequences of actions in all the previous lives the soul has lived. Will, the power of the individual personality to choose and change in the present, is placed between the forces of destiny and fate, and alone has the power to bring them into balance.

LESSON 31

Fate, will, and destiny

1. The glimpses of the mental plane that come between lives are also the source of the soul's destiny during each of its incarnations. Three primary factors—fate, will, and destiny—determine the nature of each incarnation. To understand fate, will, and destiny in general is to know the forces that shape human life. To understand your own fate, your own will, and your own destiny is to take charge of your own incarnation and to know what you can and cannot accomplish in your present life.
2. Fate is the sum of all the influences you bring to this life from previous lives. It is the factor that Eastern spiritual traditions call "karma". It is a mistake to think of fate as a matter of punishment or reward, for it is simply the rule that every action has its consequences. What you have done in previous lives has shaped the personality you have and the situations you will encounter in this life, for good or ill. Thus everything that happens to you in this life is influenced by causes you set in motion in previous lives, and your actions in this life are influencing the lives you will have in the future.
3. Some people who are aware of the influence of fate feel as though they are trapped by it, but fate is only one of the three factors that

shape human life. Destiny is another. Where fate is the legacy of the past, destiny is the pull of the future. It is the direction in which your soul is trying to move in response to its glimpses of the mental plane between lives, and it is the force that allows you to overcome the repetitive patterns set in motion by fate. Like fate, destiny plays a role in shaping the personality you have and the situations you encounter in this life.

4. The relation between your fate and your destiny has an important influence on your life. In some cases, when a series of past incarnations have been used wisely, fate and destiny point in the same direction, or in directions that are harmonious with each other. In others, fate and destiny can move in unrelated directions, or at cross purposes, or in opposition to each other. The more your fate and your destiny cooperate with each other, the easier your life will be, and the more they conflict, the more challenging your life will be

5. It is the third factor, however, that determines how the balance between fate and destiny will work out. This is will, which is your own capacity to choose. There has been a great deal of debate about whether will is free or determined, and as usual with such debates, the answer lies in the middle and varies from case to case. Your own will is always limited to some extent by the pressures of fate and destiny, and your ability to use your will also depends on how divided it is. A will that is divided among many goals has little freedom or power to accomplish anything. When the will focuses on one goal, or a set of closely related goals, it has considerable freedom and power and can transform the life of the individual for better or worse.

6. When fate and destiny pull in different directions, will holds the balance between them, and the stronger and more unified the will is, the more power it has to determine the outcome. If a strong will aligns with fate against destiny, fate overcomes destiny and the life will be spent repeating patterns of behavior passed down from previous lives, moving in circles that go nowhere. If a strong will aligns with destiny against fate, destiny overcomes fate, unproductive patterns from the past are set aside once and for all, and the soul moves toward its goal. If fate, will, and destiny pull in three different directions, the life is a constant struggle that usually accomplishes nothing and gets nowhere.

7. Three factors working together will bring fate, will, and destiny into harmony. First, wise and ethical behavior in the present incarnation

will establish favorable patterns of fate in this and future lives, and bring fate into alignment with destiny. Second, spiritual practices that are intended to develop intuition will make it easier for you to recognize destiny and align the individual will with it. Third, discipline of any kind, spiritual or otherwise, frees the will of division and gives you control over your habits of willing, so that once it is aligned with destiny, the will can act with its full strength. Any one of these, practiced consistently, can transform your incarnation utterly; all three of them practiced together open the portals of the Mysteries.

Awareness exercise

During the week you spend on this lesson, as you go about your daily activities, see if you can begin to sort out the competing influences of fate, will, and destiny in your life. Fate is easiest to see in your circumstances, especially those that resist you. Will is easiest to trace in what you actually do, not in what you think you ought to do or tell yourself you want to do. Destiny is the most difficult of the three to sort out of the background, but it often shows up most clearly in dreams and coincidences, and also in whatever talents you have, whether you have developed them or not. Explore these and see what you learn.

Affirmation

"I align my will with my destiny—and I gain mastery over my fate."

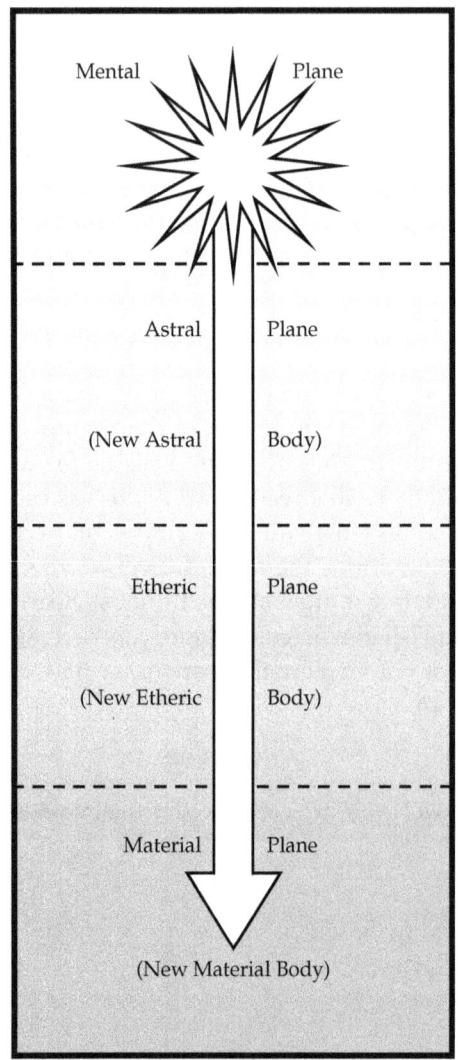

The return to material incarnation follows the same route as the dying process, but in reverse. Having absorbed as much as it can from its glimpse of the mental plane, the soul descends through the planes in order, taking on a new body on each plane, so that it is prepared to begin the adventure of its next life.

LESSON 32

Toward a new incarnation

1. Once the soul has had its glimpse of the mental plane, however brief and fragmentary or lengthy and detailed that may be, it begins to prepare for its next incarnation. If it has not yet developed its mental sheath into a mental body, it will need to descend all the way back to the material plane, to a body and a set of circumstances that are suited to its fate and its destiny. Sometimes this takes very little time, especially when the soul has recently become human and still has most of the lessons of the human kingdom before it. In other cases the soul must wait for a prolonged period before a suitable life becomes available.
2. Until a soul has developed its mental sheath to a considerable degree, it has very little choice concerning its next life. The movement toward reincarnation is more like a reflex than a conscious choice. The soul sinks back into sleep and begins to dream a new incarnation into being, and certain spiritual entities who superintend the process of reincarnation see to it that the soul passes through the necessary stages of preparation for its next life. Only when the mental sheath is well-developed can the soul begin to exercise some degree of conscious choice over the circumstances of its next life.

3. Until that point is reached, the most important influence on a soul's next incarnation is the influence of fate. Fate, as pointed out in the previous lesson, is simply the rule that every action has its consequences, and every soul must live through the consequences of its own actions in order to learn the lessons of the human stage of its evolution. Those who commit acts of violence, or cause other people to commit such acts, will suffer acts of violence in turn; those who help and heal others will be helped and healed in turn. There is no judgment involved in this process, simply the impersonal working out of cause and effect from life to life.
4. Fate can also establish connections between souls. A casual act that does harm creates no such connection—the soul of the perpetrator will suffer a corresponding act of violence in a later life, but the soul of the victim goes on to other things. When two or more souls are linked by intense passion, however, harmful acts between them can create a shared fate, which functions like a debt. When those souls reincarnate they will find themselves in a situation in which the debt can be paid. If the soul owing the debt refuses the acts that would clear away the shared fate, it will be reborn again in a similar situation as many times as necessary until the debt is paid. When two or more souls have both engaged in the kind of activities that can create such a debt, the complicated knot of fate that results can take many lives to untangle.
5. Once the mental sheath is well-developed, by contrast, it becomes possible for the soul to outgrow these connections and pay its remaining debts in a few lives, or in one. Sometimes this can be done in a single life of tremendous suffering. The kind of person who remains kind and cheerful despite a life full of profoundly painful experiences is usually someone whose soul has deliberately accepted such a life in order to clear away the burden of fate. Other souls pay their debts over several lives. In either case, once this is done, the soul can proceed without difficulty to another incarnation on the material plane, or to rise above the wheel of life and death by finishing the work of evolving a mental body.
6. Whether the soul proceeds consciously into its next life or is drawn there reflexively by the pressures of fate, the process of reincarnation is the same. First, the soul loses its awareness of the mental plane and sinks back down to the astral plane, where it gathers together the raw materials for a new astral body. The new astral body will have

many of the same characteristics as the astral body of the most recent life. When the soul spent much of its previous life playing music, for example, the new astral body will include musical patterns, which will express themselves as musical talent in the life to come. The soul of Mozart, who could play the violin brilliantly while he was still a small child, had devoted many previous lives to music; all great talents show the presence of many lives of effort in one chosen field.

7. The next step in the process of rebirth is the linking up of the soul with its new material and etheric bodies. Both of these come into being within the mother's womb, drawing on the substance of the mother's material and etheric bodies during the process of pregnancy. According to traditional lore, the moment of connection between the soul and its new bodies takes place around the time of quickening—that is, the point at which the mother begins to feel the baby move in her womb. From that point on, the baby is a fully human being, with a mental sheath and a full set of astral, etheric, and material bodies, which simply need to finish growing until they are ready for life outside the womb.

Awareness exercise

During the week you spend on this lesson, as you go about your daily activities, pay special attention to situations that have recurred over and over again in your life. Consider the possibility that they are part of the fate you have earned by your soul's actions in previous lives. Reflect on what you might have to do to accept that fate, learn from it, and go on.

Affirmation

"I learn the lessons fate is teaching me—and I pass beyond them."

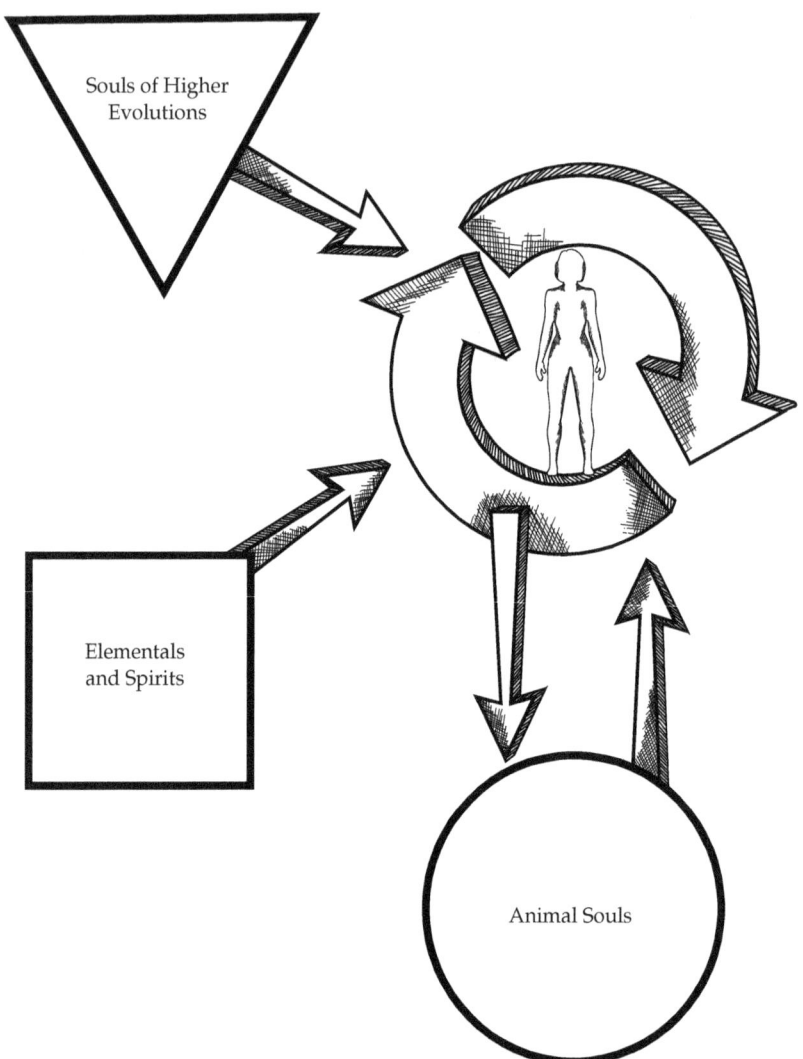

The vast majority of souls who are incarnate in human bodies have been human in their previous lives, but there are exceptions. Souls that have completed their work on the animal level are reborn in human bodies; on occasion, elementals and spirits are born in human bodies; and in special circumstances, souls belonging to higher evolutions may also be born as human beings. Under some circumstances human souls also fall back to the animal level to rise again.

LESSON 33

Reincarnation and the nonhuman

1. The process of reincarnation is not limited to human beings. Your soul was incarnated many times in mineral, plant, and animal bodies before you developed a mental sheath and began your human incarnations, and the animals, plants, and seemingly inanimate substances that surround you are all full of souls that will one day face the same challenges that you are facing today. Nor is the barrier between human and nonhuman lives impassable. Animal souls that have evolved a mental sheath can cross into the human level, and it is also possible to go in the other direction, sinking back into the animal kingdom.
2. Most souls, once they reach the human level, remain there until they have evolved a mental body and are ready to leave the wheel of birth and death. It is possible, however, for a soul that has reached the human level to fail so badly at the process of being human that it falls back to the animal level. The mental sheath is fragile at first, and a soul that repeatedly rejects its own awareness of the mental plane—its own inner knowledge of meaning, value, and purpose—will disintegrate its mental sheath. Once this happens, the soul is that of an animal, and will be reborn as an animal until it can evolve a new mental sheath after many more lives.

3. This retrograde motion of souls, from the human kingdom back to the animal kingdom, happens most often at certain phases in the cycles of history. These cycles move between periods of greater spirituality and low population, on the one hand, and greater materialism and high population, on the other. It is in these latter periods, when materialism is at its peak and it is easiest for souls to lose track of whatever knowledge they might have of the mental plane, that falling back to the animal level becomes most common. We are in such a period at present.
4. Periods of greater materialism and high population are also periods in which a larger share of the human population has just risen out of the animal kingdom. Just as souls descend and then ascend the planes in seven swarms, of which we belong to the fourth, within each swarm there are greater and smaller groups of souls, which tend to move through the evolutionary journey together. When a large group of souls rises up more or less together to the human level, the result is a parallel increase in population and materialism, since the newly arrived souls are still mostly animal at first, with only a very slight influence from the mental plane. Thus it is easy in such times for souls to lose their way entirely and drift back into the animal stage of evolution.
5. It is also possible under some circumstances for souls that are not part of our fourth swarm to become incarnate in human bodies. This most often happens with elementals who have had repeated interactions with human beings. Most children born with elemental souls die young, and those few who reach adulthood have relatively short lives. Since elementals lack a divine spark, they are without conscience, and since their etheric and astral bodies are highly charged by human standards, they tend to produce violent passions and hatreds in ordinary humans who encounter them. Such children are most often born in phases of history where population is high, since human bodies are readily available at such times.
6. Finally, it is possible under certain very special circumstances for a being of a more advanced stage of evolution, such as a Lord of Mind, to become incarnate in a human body. When this happens is determined not by ordinary historical cycles but by the will of the Solar Logos and the requirements of human evolution. Children born with a soul from a more advanced stage of evolution tend to display unusual wisdom and intelligence from a very early age, enter into

life with a clear sense of the purpose they have come to accomplish, carry out that purpose in the face of all opposition, and die promptly, often by violence, once it is complete.

7. All these interactions between nonhuman souls and the human world happen from time to time, but the only one that happens routinely is the process by which animal souls develop rudimentary mental sheaths and are born into human bodies. The loss of a mental sheath by a formerly human soul is rare; the birth of a child with an elemental soul is rarer, and the birth of a child with a soul from a higher evolution happens only once in a very long time. It is helpful to be aware of these possibilities to understand the nature of reincarnation, but out of all the people you will meet in your present incarnation, most will have been human for at least one life, a few may be on their first human life, and it is unlikely that even one will have a truly nonhuman soul.

Awareness exercise

During the week you spend on this lesson, spend time now and again thinking of the journey your own soul has made up the winding stair of evolution, from your first incarnation in the mineral kingdom to the life you are living today. Think about what it might have been like when you had your first human incarnation, and had to cope for the first time with all the details of human existence that come naturally to you now. Then try to imagine what it will be like when you finish evolving a mental body and rise to the level beyond humanity.

Affirmation

"I welcome new souls to the human level—as I prepare to rise above it."

Nations, like individuals, are born, grow up, mature, age, and die. Under some circumstances, their group souls can reincarnate as the souls of new nations. Each nation also has its own fate, will, and destiny. Every nation expresses some specific way of being human; it thrives while it follows the promptings of its destiny, and it perishes when its actions result in a burden of fate too great for it to carry and survive.

LESSON 34

The life and death of nations

1. Like individual human beings, human nations have life cycles. They are born, grow up, reach maturity, grow old, die, and are reborn. The cycles of history mentioned in the previous lesson include the life cycles of nations, as well as vaster cycles that define the ages of the world, which will be discussed shortly. All these cycles have their own importance in occult philosophy, and so should be discussed at this point.
2. It is common to describe a nation as a group of people who share a common language, culture, and history, and (sometimes) have political control over a land area. All these things are outward expressions of an inward reality. From the standpoint of occult philosophy, a nation is a group of people who share a common group soul. As mentioned earlier, national group souls are much less powerful and influential than the group souls of plants and animals, but they can offer the people of their nation some degree of guidance in the complexities of life. National habits, customs, and attitudes are among the things that national group souls maintain.
3. Like elementals, national group souls have no divine sparks—this is why individuals have a conscience but nations have none. They

function mostly on the astral, and their material and etheric bodies consist of the material and etheric bodies of the people who belong to them. There are many degrees of belonging to a national group soul, ranging from those people who feel themselves intensely to be part of the national community to those for whom nationality means nothing, and including those who belong by birth or personal commitment to more than one nation. For this reason the real boundaries of a nation can never be drawn on a map.

4. Just as a human soul cannot reincarnate until a suitable human body is ready for it, a national group soul cannot reincarnate until a group of people is ready to become a nation. Just as a human soul is not created by its material and etheric bodies, but descends into those bodies from above, a national group soul is not created by the people who belong to it, but descends into manifestation in the same way that a soul descends into incarnation, entering into bodies provided for it on the material and etheric planes. Like people, nations can be killed by accident or violence, but each nation that lives long enough has its childhood, its youth, its adulthood, its maturity, its old age, and its death.

5. The life cycles of nations move from spirituality to materialism, as discussed in the previous lesson. Nations begin their history in a condition of low population and high spirituality. As they grow and mature, they gradually change to a condition of high population and high materiality, in which the pursuit of material wealth and power becomes the focus of national effort. Those nations that survive this stage and reach old age gradually settle back into a condition of low population and high spirituality. The national group soul changes accordingly, passing from a child's faith in traditional religious beliefs through an adulthood focused on material realities to an old age in which the spiritual world again draws close.

6. National group souls can be reborn after an interval. In some cases, this happens in the same place and among the same ethnic and cultural groups. The national group soul of China, for example, has been reborn repeatedly in the same part of the planet across five thousand years of history. In others, a national group soul can reincarnate in a different place and among ethnic and cultural groups unrelated to those it once gathered to itself, but it can be recognized by the recurrence of old habits, images, and attitudes. Since the beginning of the nineteenth century, for example, astute observers of the United States

have noticed similarities linking that nation with ancient Rome. The most likely explanation is that the Roman group soul was reincarnated on American soil when the United States became a nation.

7. The guiding influence of the national group soul is most important for souls that have recently become human and are still used to being directed by a group soul, as they were in their animal incarnations. As souls begin to develop their mental sheaths and take control over their own evolution, the guidance of the group soul is less necessary, but at this point the relationship begins to reverse: souls that perceive meaning, purpose, and value on the mental plane start to influence the national group soul. The most noteworthy eras in national life are always those in which an unusually large number of citizens have achieved some awareness of the mental plane.

Awareness exercise

During the week you spend on this lesson, as you go about your daily activities, notice the influence of your national culture on your own life and the lives of people around you. Think about how the details of your life would be different if you lived in another country. (If you don't know what the differences would be, see if you can find information on this online or in books written for travelers.) Try to sense the role that your own national background plays in your thoughts and feelings.

Affirmation

"The group soul of my nation guides me—and I help guide it in return."

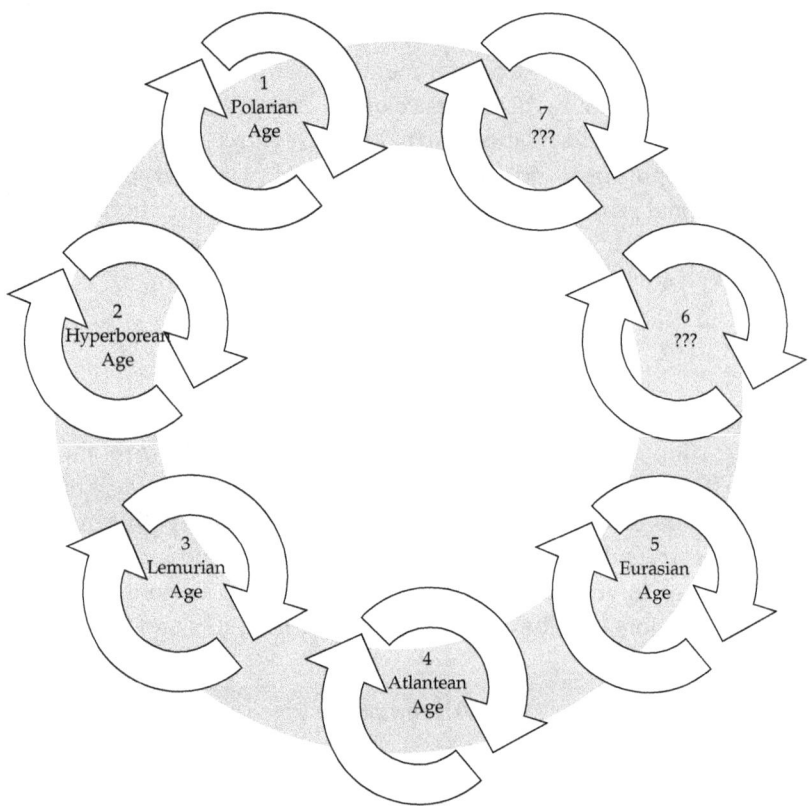

The age of the world in which we live is the fifth age of humanity. All of recorded history from the first mud brick cities in the Middle East belongs to this fifth age, which may be called the Eurasian age on account of the major centers of civilization during it. Our age still has thousands of years to run, and after it ends, there will be two more ages before our species has completed its work on this planet.

LESSON 35

Ages of the world

1. On a far greater time scale than the rise and fall of nations is the sequence of ages of the world. According to the teachings of occult philosophy, the whole lifespan of the human race in its material incarnation on Earth is divided into seven ages. Each age lasts for many thousands of years, and an interval of several thousand years separates each age from the ages before and after it. Each age proceeds, in the way already discussed, from low population and high spirituality to high population and high materialism, and back to low population and high spirituality. We currently live roughly halfway through the fifth age of the world.
2. Very little is known at the present time about the first two ages of the world, which are traditionally called the Polarian and Hyperborean ages. They are thought to have taken place before the beginning of the last ice age, when the Arctic Ocean was still ice-free and tropical heat extended much further north and south than it does today. The land areas central to human civilization in those ages were located near the poles, possibly in areas that are now covered by ice. Even at the peaks of those ages, world population was a tiny fraction of what it is today, and the nations of those times had very simple material

technologies compared to those we now have, but their spiritual technologies were far in advance of ours.

3. The third age of the world is traditionally called the Lemurian age, and more is known about it. It flourished early in the last ice age, when sea level was hundreds of feet lower than it is today. The land area central to human civilization in that age was located in what are now shallow seas south and east of Asia, on a now-flooded land mass the size of India. The countless islands that now rise out of the ocean between Asia and Australia were once the mountains of Lemuria. In Lemurian times the balance between spiritual and material technologies had begun to tip further in a material direction but had not yet gone as far into matter as we have.

4. The fourth age of the world, the one before ours, is traditionally called the Atlantean age, and more is known about it than about the ones before it. It flourished toward the end of the last ice age, and it ended as the great glaciers melted and caused the worldwide coastal flooding recalled in the legends of Atlantis. The land area central to human civilization in that era was located around both sides of the northern Atlantic basin, centered on several large islands (now underwater) east of North America. The Atlantean age had advanced material technologies, but those were reserved for the use of priestly elites rather than being spread through the population as ours are. It was through the misuse of those technologies, according to occult tradition, that the Atlantean age ended beneath rising seas.

5. The Atlantean age ended around 9600 BC. It was followed by an interval that lasted around five thousand years, during which global population was very low and most Atlantean technologies were lost. Only when the seas stopped rising and the climate stabilized did new civilizations rise in Egypt and Sumer, marking the beginning of the fifth age of the world, the age in which we live. Our age has had several names in occult writings. Since the previous ages have all been named after the land area that was central to human civilization at that time, and since the center of human civilization in this age has been the belt of urban societies extending from China west through India and the Middle East to Europe, it can be called the Eurasian age.

6. After the Eurasian age is over, and an interval passes, a new age of the world will begin. We can know only a little about the sixth age. Some occult writings, drawing on psychic visions, suggest that the

center of human civilization in that age will be along the eastern shores of the Pacific Ocean, in what is now North America, but that is little more than a guess at this point. Many thousands of years later, that age will come to its end, and after another interval, the seventh age will begin. We know nothing yet about this last age of human civilization on Earth.

7. It is worth remembering that the entire sweep of recorded history, from the first mud brick towns of the ancient Middle East five thousand years ago to the skyscrapers of today, is only the first half or so of the fifth age of the world. Our age has reached its peak but it still has many thousands of years to go, and many changes to pass through, before it ends. During that time, nations and cultures will rise and fall, as they have done all through this and every previous age—ancient Egypt and imperial Rome did not last forever, and neither will our civilization.

Awareness exercise

During the week you spend on this lesson, think about the vision of the past that has been sketched out in this lesson. Many people nowadays like to believe that ours is the first civilization ever to achieve advanced technology. How does it change the way you think about your life and the world to consider the possibility that there were other advanced civilizations long before our time, and that our species has a history far longer than current records indicate?

Affirmation

"In all the vast reaches of time—this moment alone belongs to me."

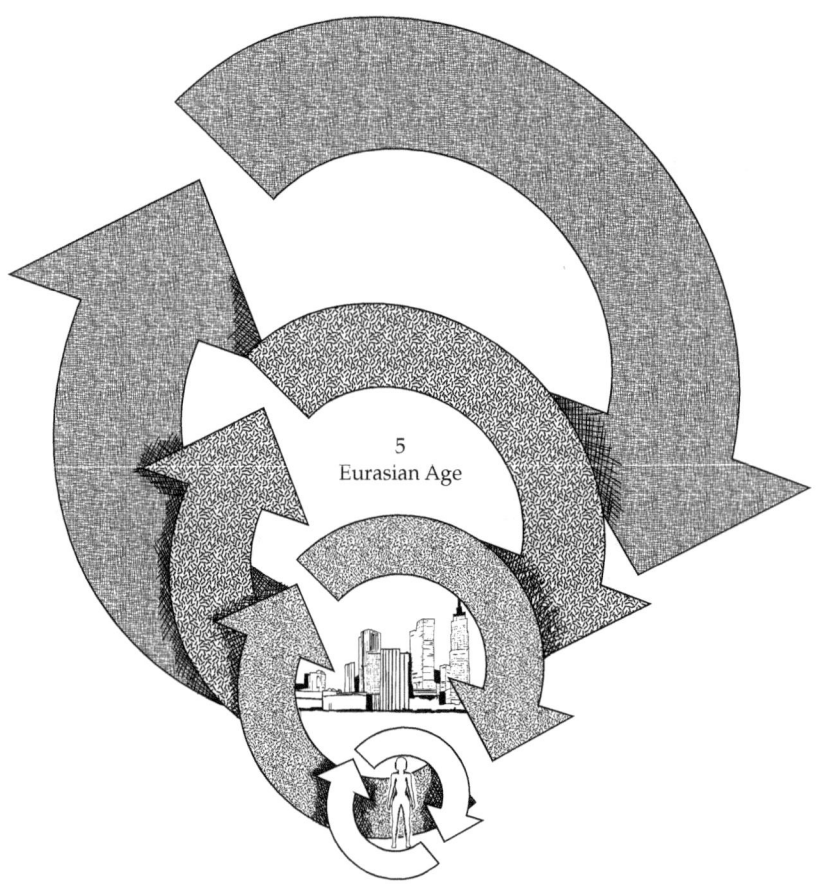

5
Eurasian Age

The life cycle of the individual human being takes place in a world defined by other, greater life cycles. Nations, ages of the world, and species are born, grow, mature, age, and die as people do, and the fates, wills, and destinies of individuals are caught up in the vast cycles of fate, will, and destiny that shape these collective phenomena.

LESSON 36

The cycles of time

1. In our time, the fifth age of the world is roughly halfway through its life cycle, in its period of highest population and highest materialism. The human population of this planet is very high, but scientists have already reported that birth rates are dropping, heralding the time when population will peak and begin to decline worldwide. The technology of our age still has room to develop somewhat further, but the rate of innovation has been declining for many years as the cost of research goes up. Here, too, the peak is coming into sight before us.
2. This is not the way most people like to think about the future nowadays. Just as it's popular to imagine that our civilization is the first ever to have advanced technology, it's popular to believe that our technology will become ever more powerful, until it either transforms human life utterly or annihilates us all. Those paired visions of utopia or oblivion are pervasive in our time, and make it difficult for most people to think about other possibilities. The fact that so many dates for the arrival of utopia or oblivion have gone past without incident has done little to improve matters.

3. From the standpoint of occultism, these visions of utopia and oblivion are rooted in a dim sense of our destiny, but that dim sense has been misunderstood due to cultural factors and the pervasive material-mindedness of our time. Both visions start from the vague awareness that human beings will not continue to inhabit the Earth forever. The vision of utopia, which so often focuses on imagery of space travel, grasps also that in some sense we will rise above the Earth and leave it behind. The vision of oblivion, which so often focuses on imagery of mass death, grasps also that at some point in the future our species will no longer exist. Both these visions are partly accurate and partly mistaken.

4. What believers in both these visions of the future are perceiving dimly is that they, along with every other human being, have a material body and experience the material plane only until they finish the process of evolving a mental body. Once that process is finished, they will rise above the material plane, though rockets will not be required for that ascent. Once that process is finished, equally, humans in material bodies will no longer exist on Earth, though global cataclysms will not be required for that to happen. Through the natural unfolding of human evolution, each of us will proceed on to the next stage of our journey.

5. Yet this transformation, like the rest of the soul's journey down through the planes of being and back up again, is individual, not collective. Each of us must go through the processes of evolution individually, by our own efforts; we can receive assistance from other souls incarnate as human beings, and also from souls that have moved ahead of us in the evolutionary journey, but each of us must do the most important part of the work ourselves. This is one of two crucial points missed by the visions of collective transformation; they insist that the world will change, so that we don't have to.

6. The other point missed by these visions is that the current state of human affairs, with all its griefs and troubles, is not a mistake, much less a temporary condition that can be fixed. Human life is what it is because it contains all the experiences that our souls need in order to pass through the great transition to objective existence on the mental plane. The hurt and heartbreak and tragedy of human life, as well as its joys and its possibilities for accomplishment, are necessary parts of our journey through this evolutionary level. When we have learned what we need to learn from those experiences, we will have

evolved a mental body and we will rise above the cycle of life and death. Meanwhile, other souls who need those lessons will rise up to take our places on the human level of existence.

7. Each of us will die someday, and go on to other incarnations. Our civilization will decline and fall someday, and leave room for new civilizations to arise. The fifth age of the world will come to an end someday, and a sixth age will rise after the usual interval. Our species will finish its time on this planet someday, and there will be other intelligent species after us, just as (according to occult tradition) there were other intelligent species before us. The solar system itself has a life cycle with a beginning and an end. Learning to live within these cycles of time, rather than vainly waiting for someone or something else to change the world for our benefit, is an important part of the wisdom that occultism teaches

Awareness exercise

During the week you spend on this lesson, think about the vision of the future that has been sketched out in this lesson. Many people nowadays like to believe that our civilization is destined to endure forever and spread itself throughout space. How does it change the way you think about your life and the world to consider the possibility that ours is simply one of many civilizations, each with its life cycle, and that the current age of the world has already passed its peak and will wind down from here?

Affirmation

"The future of my soul—depends on my own choices and actions."

UNIT FOUR

THE WAY OF OCCULTISM

The teachings of occultism descend to us from the distant past. Early in the present age of the world, those teachings were first formulated in ancient Egypt. They were enriched and transmitted to a wider world by the philosophers of Greece and then, after the turmoil of the middle ages, revived and reorganized by the great minds of the Renaissance. As an occultist you are an inheritor of the lore and labors of all those who came before you.

LESSON 37

The sources of occultism

1. Long ago, at the dawn of the Polarian age, when souls with rudimentary mental sheaths first incarnated in a species of upright ape and became the first human beings, they faced the same perplexities about the seen and unseen worlds discussed in the first lesson in this book. Their first uncertain wonderings about the nature of the unseen began the process from which today's occult traditions eventually evolved. Every human society since that distant time has contributed to the growth of occultism in one way or another, giving rise to the rich and complex body of lore that occultists study today.
2. Not all of that lore originated with human beings. Early in the history of every nation, when its population is low and its spirituality high, the Lords of Mind reach out to the people of that nation, bringing about an era of prophets and visionaries whose work helps give the nation or the age its initial guidance. Late in the history of every nation, when population is again low and spirituality high, the Lords of Mind reach out again to the nation, and help the loremasters and initiates of the nation's traditions synthesize their teachings so these can be passed onto nations to come. These same processes take

place on a much larger scale at the beginning and ending of civilizations and of ages of the world.
3. In the present fifth age of the world, the first great center of occultism was Egypt. According to occult tradition, Egypt began its long history as a surviving colony of one of the last civilizations of the Atlantean age. Once a new age of the world dawned, Egyptian initiates spread the teachings of occultism, first south into Africa, and then east to India. Finally, in the last years of Egyptian civilization, seekers of wisdom from Greece received the teachings in Egypt and took those back with them to Europe.
4. Pythagoras, the most important of these seekers of wisdom, traveled the known world in search of occult lore. To his school at Crotona, in what is now Italy, most modern Western traditions of occultism can trace at least some of their heritage. Egypt was not the only source of occult teachings in the fifth age of the world, however, nor was the school of Pythagoras the only center from which occultism spread. Several other parts of the world preserved legacies from the Atlantean age, and according to tradition, a few still retained teachings from the Lemurian age. By the time of Pythagoras most nations had their own occult traditions, taught in temple schools to students who passed stringent tests of their fitness.
5. About two thousand years ago, that began to change. The bitter class conflicts of the ancient world led to the rise of religions of the poor, which rejected occultism in favor of beliefs that claimed to offer salvation to everyone. Over the centuries that followed, as those religions took power across Europe and the Middle East, the temple schools were shut down and the first waves of violent persecutions followed. Thereafter, for more than a thousand years, occultism in those regions of the world struggled for survival, now and then flourishing openly under the protection of a wise ruler, but more often passed on in secret by people who risked their reputations or their lives for the sake of occult wisdom.
6. In Europe during the Renaissance, as the grip of religious orthodoxy failed, occultism flourished in public as it had not done since the fall of the ancient world. The newly invented printing press allowed occult texts to be circulated freely, and great strides were made in piecing together the scattered wisdom from before the age of persecutions. The deepening materialism of the age, however, eventually smothered the occult revival of the Renaissance, and for many years

thereafter occult teachings were again preserved by small groups of people who met in secret to share what they knew and keep the flame of the secret wisdom alight.
7. As a student of occultism today you share in the age-old heritage preserved by those small groups and the traditions they recovered. The teachings you study and the exercises you practice were assembled out of older materials to help you accomplish the work of human evolution, and you share with all occultists in the modern world the responsibility of helping to see to it that the wisdom of the past is delivered into the waiting hands of the future.

Awareness exercise

During the week you spend on this lesson, think about the long history of occultism, and make an effort to see yourself as part of that history. Imagine occultists in the distant future thinking back to our time, far in their past, and thinking about those from whom their traditions descend; imagine occultists in the distant past thinking forward to our time, far in their future, and thinking about those to whom their traditions would someday come. How does that affect the way you understand your own practice of occultism?

Affirmation

"I am one of the heirs—of the occult teachings of the ages."

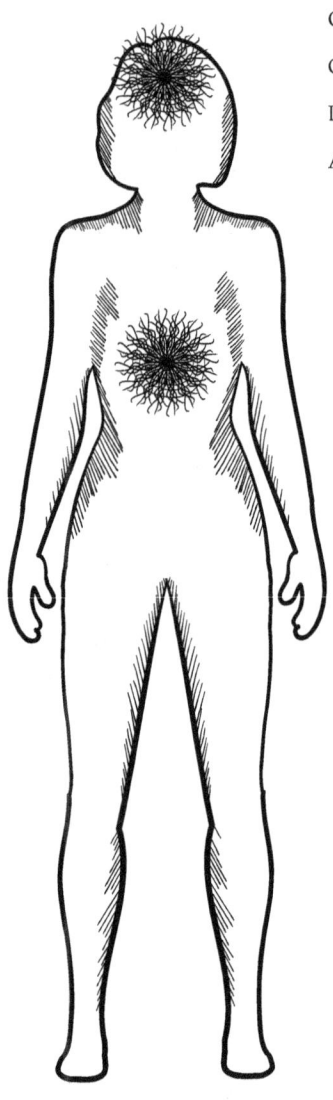

Objective Mind:

Oriented to the outer world

Linked to the personality

Awake during incarnation

Subjective Mind:

Oriented to the inner world

Linked to the soul

Asleep and dreaming during incarnation

Each of us has two minds, the objective mind oriented toward the outer world and the subjective mind oriented toward the inner world. The objective mind is the mind of the personality and is awake, during waking hours, while we are incarnate. The subjective mind is the mind of the sleeping soul, and remains in a dream state during incarnation. Many of the practices of occult training focus on opening channels of communication between the two minds.

LESSON 38

Subjective and objective minds

1. In order to make sense of the way of occult training, it is necessary to understand the distinction between your subjective and objective minds, which were mentioned earlier in this series of lessons but not explored in detail. Your objective mind is the mind that you are using right now as you read these words and think about what they mean. It is called "objective" because it faces outward, toward the world of objects that surrounds you. Your objective mind is located in your head, or more precisely the part of your astral body that overlaps with the head of your physical body. Many people nowadays call it "the conscious mind."
2. Your subjective mind is a little harder to understand, because our culture pays very little attention to it. Your subjective mind faces inward, toward you as a subject, rather than outward, toward a world full of objects. It is the mind you think with in dreams and daydreams, and it is the source of intuitions and "gut feelings." It is also the mind that keeps you alive—it tells your heart to beat, your lungs to breathe, your stomach to digest food, and so on. It is located in your solar plexus, the area right behind your stomach, or more

precisely in that area in your astral body. Many people nowadays call it "the subconscious mind."

3. These two minds have an important relationship with your personality and your soul. Your personality, the set of habits of thinking, feeling, and acting that you have developed in this incarnation, is centered in your head and relates most closely to your objective mind. Your soul, your real self, which existed ages before your present material body was born and will continue to exist ages after your present material body has died, is centered in your solar plexus and relates most closely to your subjective mind. In incarnation, as you have learned, your soul is in effect asleep, while your personality is awake. You can think of the subjective mind, in fact, as your sleeping soul.

4. When you are thinking with your objective mind, which you do most of the time when you are awake, you pay attention to the world of objects around you and very often do not notice what is going on inside you. There are times when this is appropriate and even necessary, since learning to attend to the world around you is an important part of the work you are doing in this incarnation. It is important, however, to attend to the subjective mind and the inner world as well, and this is a central theme of occult practice. Disciplines such as ritual, meditation, and divination are ways of working with the subjective mind.

5. To turn your attention at regular intervals to the subjective mind, through practices like those just named, has several effects that are important in occult training. First, when you turn your attention to your subjective mind, you can perceive physical tensions and other unhealthy states that you may not notice when you attend solely to your objective mind. Learning to relax unnecessary tensions, to breathe deeply and steadily, to allow healthful influences to enter into your body and to allow unhealthy influences to leave your body, are all steps to better physical, emotional, and mental health.

6. All these are benefits on the material plane. On the etheric and astral planes, subtle connections link the solar plexus center with other energy centers in the body, and especially with the pineal center in the middle of the brain. Some methods for awakening the subtle centers can only be done safely under very tightly restricted conditions, but regularly turning the attention to the subjective mind and working with it in occult exercises awakens the solar plexus center,

and then the other centers, in a safe and balanced manner. The most important result of that awakening is the development of intuition, which as you have learned is the central goal of occult training.

7. The development of intuition leads to wisdom, which we can define as the interior sense of truth, guided by dawning awareness on the mental plane that makes it possible to live in creative harmony with the world. At the same time, it opens the door to revelation, which we can define as the sudden attainment of a glimpse of the mental plane. Ultimately, the development of intuition leads to enlightenment, which cannot be defined, but can be described tentatively as a state in which wisdom and revelation are permanent conditions of the soul. This is the summit of the occult path.

Awareness exercise

During the week you spend on this lesson, pay attention to the way you relate to the two worlds described above, the outer world perceived by the objective mind and the inner world perceived by the subjective mind. Notice which of them receives most of your attention, and also what feelings and beliefs you have about the two minds and the worlds they perceive.

Affirmation

"I awaken my intuition—by balancing my inner and outer worlds."

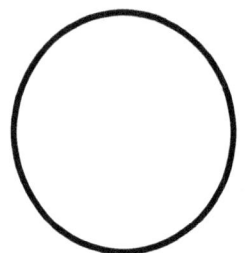

Illumination:
the work of unfolding the potentials
of practice and experiencing higher
states of awareness

Interiorization:
the work of interacting with
your subjective mind and
inner world in practice

Preparation:
the work of learning the
exercises of your tradition and
establishing a regular practice

The three stages of preparation, interiorization, and illumination are encountered by every student of occultism, not once but many times. With each practice you take up, and in each stage of that practice as it unfolds itself to you, there is the stage of patient application to the basics, the stage of struggling with ingrained habits and the deep structures of yourself, and the stage of awakening to new possibilities.

LESSON 39

The process of occult training

1. Most people in the modern Western world pay close attention to their objective minds and largely ignore their subjective minds. This is a habit that has to be overcome by every student of occultism. Most of the practices taught in occult schools have many functions, but one of them is to teach you to pay more attention to your subjective mind and your inner life. By doing this you begin the process of developing intuition and set yourself on the path that leads ultimately to wisdom, revelation, and enlightenment.
2. Different occult schools use different exercises. The practice of discursive meditation, which is taught in the Appendix to this book, is common to most occult schools, but not all, and methods of meditation vary somewhat from school to school. This book teaches philosophy rather than practice, and so no attempt will be made here to explore the details of how different occult exercises function. If you wish to understand those details, the best way is to practice the exercises of your tradition regularly over a long period, and use study, reflection, and meditation to explore how each exercise helps to shape your consciousness and personality over time.

3. The differences between traditions and schools of occultism are mirrored by the differences among the bodies and minds of individual students. Each person who comes to the occult path brings a unique pattern of experiences in this and previous lives, and as a result no two people will have exactly the same experience while studying and practicing occultism. Yet we are all souls on the human level of manifestation, developing our mental sheaths into mental bodies, and this shared situation allows certain generalizations to be made. The way of occult training can therefore be divided, for most people, into three broad phases.

4. The first of these steps is the phase of preparation, which involves learning the various exercises that are assigned to you by the tradition you are following or the school in which you are studying, establishing a regular practice with each of them, and picking up enough basic familiarity with the way the exercises work that you no longer need to concentrate on getting all the details right and can begin work on using the exercises for their intended purposes. In this phase of occult training, the objective mind takes the lead and does essentially all the work, and the subjective mind remains largely unaffected by the exercises.

5. The second step is the phase of interiorization, in which the exercises you are doing turn your attention toward the subjective mind. In this phase, you become increasingly aware of the world within you and must come to terms with what you find there. As your practices become habitual, they begin to have a significant effect on the subjective mind, which typically responds at first by trying to shake off the unfamiliar influence. This is the phase in which your practice is constantly interrupted by itches, stray thoughts, sleepiness, forgetfulness, or any of a hundred other obstacles. During this time your objective and subjective minds must struggle their way toward a new balance, and you will need patience and a sense of humor to get through the process gracefully.

6. The third step is the phase of illumination. In this phase your subjective mind comes to terms with the work of occult training, and begins to cooperate with it, applying its own deeper powers to occult practice. The exercises stop being something you have to struggle to complete, and they begin to unfold their potentials as vehicles for expanded awareness. It is in this phase that intuition most often

becomes active, at least for a time, and the first stirrings of wisdom and revelation commonly appear.
7. The phase of illumination then gives way to a renewed phase of preparation as your subjective mind becomes used to the exercises and settles again into a routine. This is often irritating to beginning students, but each such cycle marks a new stage of growth and the development of new capacities in yourself. You can expect to cycle through the three phases many times over the course of your occult training, and each cycle will take you further and unfold more of your potential for wisdom, revelation, and enlightenment.

Awareness exercise

During the week you spend on this lesson, assess your own occult practices, whatever those happen to be. See if you can identify whether you are in the stage of preparation, interiorization, or illumination. It is possible that you will be at one stage with one exercise and at a different stage with another exercise.

Affirmation

"Each stage of the work I pass through—is a step toward enlightenment."

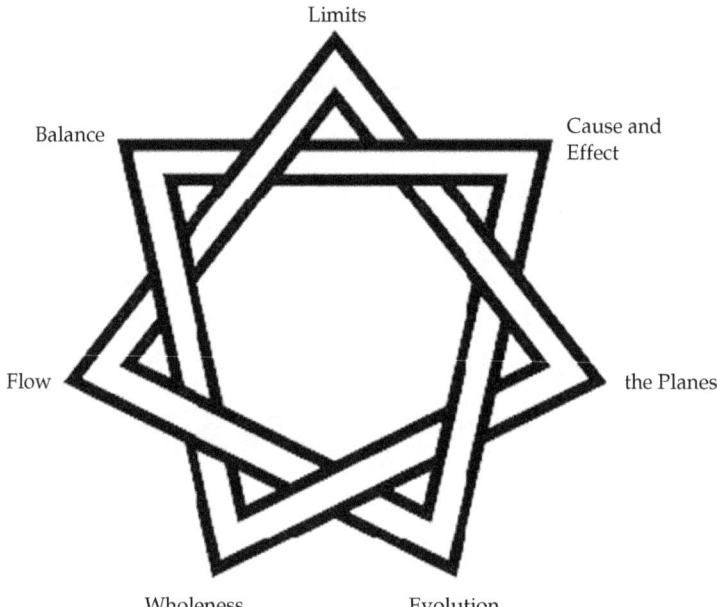

These seven spiritual laws—wholeness, flow, balance, limits, cause and effect, the planes, and evolution—provide touchstones for your spiritual path and your life as a whole. Recognize them and work with them, and they become keys to power; ignore them or pretend that they do not matter, and they become barriers to your efforts and sources of failure and unhappiness.

LESSON 40

Seven spiritual laws

1. The lessons you have already studied have covered a great deal of ground, starting from the basic principles of occultism and proceeding through a great many details concerning the universe, the individual soul, and their relationships in life and death. Some of these teachings have obvious applications to your life and your inner development, while others have subtler lessons to teach. It can be a challenge to sum up all this information into patterns that allow you to apply it in practice.
2. For this reason occult teachers have very often condensed the basic principles of occult philosophy into seven laws, principles, or maxims. Why seven? Partly, psychologists have found that most people find it easy to remember up to seven things, and much harder to remember a longer list. Still, there is a deeper reason. A sevenfold order is found all through the cosmos. The cosmos has seven cosmic planes, our solar system has seven planes, there are seven swarms of souls in the life of the solar system, and the evolution of our species on Earth takes place over seven ages, and so on. A set of seven laws therefore meshes well with the order of the cosmos.

3. The seven laws we will be studying in the lessons ahead are the Law of Wholeness, the Law of Flow, the Law of Balance, the Law of Limits, the Law of Cause and Effect, the Law of the Planes, and the Law of Evolution. While each of these laws will receive attention over the weeks to come, you can take a first step in understanding by thinking about what each of these concepts means. What is wholeness? What is flow? What is balance, and so on through the list—and what does it teach about the cosmos to say that these seven concepts are basic principles that shape everything that exists?
4. If you read other books of occult philosophy you will find that they quite often give different lists of the seven occult laws or principles. This does not mean that one set is right and the others are wrong. Rather, each set of laws is meant to direct the student's attention to specific patterns at work in the macrocosm and microcosm. Not all systems of occult practice benefit from attention to the same points, and not all historical periods suffer from the same unbalanced and unhelpful patterns of thought.
5. The lists of seven laws that were most popular in the twentieth century, and can be found in books published then, were drawn from psychology. At that time, the rigidly materialist philosophy that was common all over the industrial world convinced many people to ignore their own inner lives and concentrate on the objective mind to an even greater extent than today. Occult teachers in that era therefore focused on psychological principles to help their students begin to turn their attention to the subjective mind and understand themselves better.
6. Though the focus on the objective mind remains, the efforts of occult teachers and psychologists were successful, and most people are more aware of their own minds and inner lives than they were a century ago. Yet this has driven an imbalance of its own, because too many people now are convinced that human beings are not part of the natural world and can do whatever they want to their surroundings without consequences. For this reason among others, the laws or principles presented here come from the science of ecology, which studies how living beings relate to their environments.
7. Ecology has often been misunderstood in recent years, and even more often distorted to serve various all-too-human interests. As you proceed through the lessons to come, therefore, it is important not to confuse the principles being discussed with misunderstandings you

may have picked up from popular culture or the media. The laws of ecology are not political slogans or moral preachments. They are simply statements of what is true about the world, and they apply to all the planes of being, not just to the material plane. Understand them and learn to work with them, and they can become sources of wisdom and power in your life.

Awareness exercise

During the week you spend on this lesson, spend one day being aware of each of the seven concepts referenced in the names of the seven laws: wholeness, flow, balance, limits, cause and effect, the planes of being, and evolution. On the day you spend considering wholeness, for example, as you go about your daily activities, notice how everything you encounter is part of a larger whole. On the day you spend considering flow, notice how many things around you are flowing, quickly or slowly. (Did you know that glass is a liquid, and that windows gradually flow downward over the years?) Do this with each of the concepts listed above, and see how that experience shapes the way you understand your world.

Affirmation

"I am part of the cosmos—and I thrive by knowing its laws."

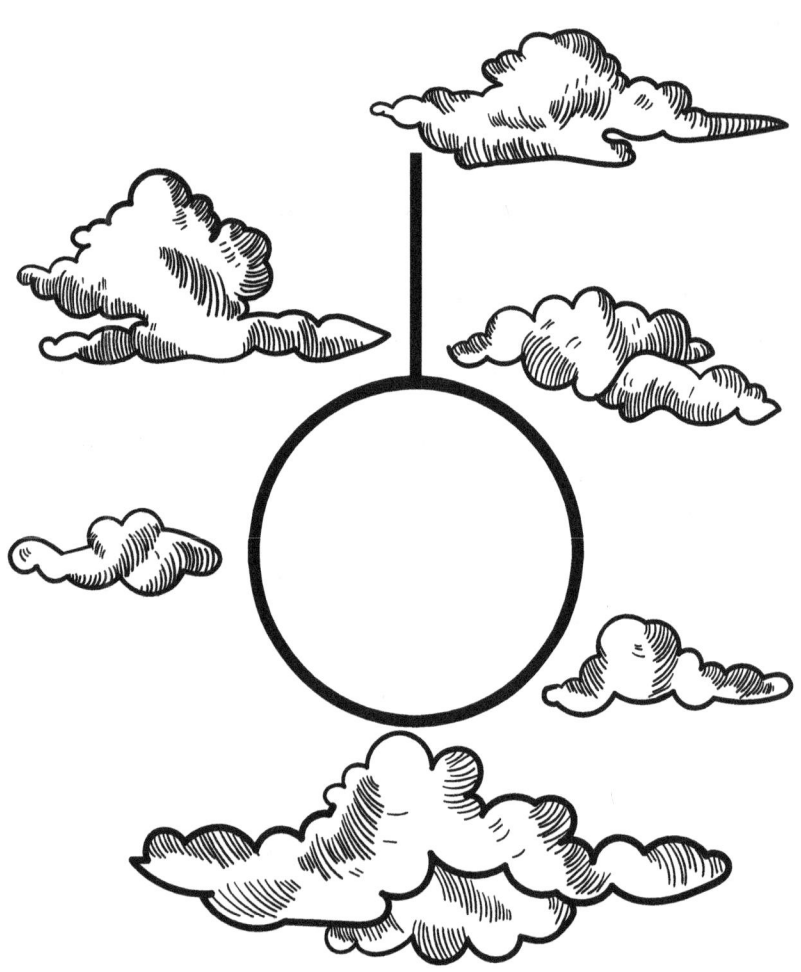

The first law is the Law of Wholeness, and states that all things are whole systems and also parts of other whole systems. Nothing in the Cosmos stands alone by itself. Everything is part of the whole, depends on the whole, and contributes to the whole. To work effectively with anything in the Cosmos it is necessary to take its connections to the whole Cosmos into account.

LESSON 41

The law of wholeness

1. One of the great lessons that souls must learn as they make their way through the transitional human stage of existence is that nothing stands apart from the rest of the cosmos in any way that matters. Just as each part of your material body depends on the body's other organs to live and thrive, every thing and being in the cosmos depends on other things and beings. This insight can be summed up in the Law of Wholeness.
2. The Law of Wholeness can be expressed this way: "Everything that exists is part of a whole system and depends on the health of the whole system for its own existence. It thrives only if the whole system thrives, and it cannot harm the whole system without harming itself."
3. The phrase "whole system" repeats no less than four times in this law, and deserves close attention. What is a system? To ecologists, a system is a group of things that interact with one another more than any of them interact with things outside the system. Think of the organs in your material body—the heart, the stomach, the lungs, the brain, and so on. Each of these is linked by a constant stream of interactions through the circulatory system, the nervous system, and more. Some of them also interact with things outside your body—the stomach

digests food, the lungs take in air, the brain processes information—but each of them is more closely tied in with your other organs, and more strongly affected by those organs, than they are with things outside your body. This is a good example of a system.

4. What the Law of Wholeness teaches is that everything belongs to systems the way that your organs belong to your body. More to the point, everything belongs to many systems. You belong to a family, a nation, a species, a swarm of souls, a planet, a solar system, and the cosmos. Anything that affects one of these things affects you, too, and everything that affects you affects all these things, maybe in a small way, maybe in a larger one. When a poet wrote "thou canst not stir a flower without troubling of a star," he was expressing the Law of Wholeness in memorable verse.

5. The Law uses the phrase "whole system" rather than "system" alone because it is such a common habit of people to notice the existence of systems and then act as though this or that part of the system doesn't matter or doesn't really belong. You may have noticed that many families have their "black sheep," the family member no one wants to talk about or deal with. Other groups have their black sheep, too. Study the whole system without letting your own assumptions get in the way and it very often becomes clear that the black sheep fills an essential role in the family or the group—for example, getting angry at the black sheep may be an acceptable way to avoid dealing with family problems that no one wants to discuss. The phrase "whole system" is there to remind us that everything in the system must be taken into account.

6. Accepting the Law of Wholeness in no way requires you to deny the value of the individual or the importance of personal freedom. It simply requires you to recognize that everything you do affects the cosmos around you. If you close your eyes to how your actions influence the whole systems of which you are a part, you can expect to be blindsided by the consequences. Choose to hate, even if you never let yourself express your hatred, and that choice will radiate outwards through all the planes you influence, and make the world a little more hateful. Choose to love, and the reverse is true.

7. This may seem at first glance like a burden, but if it is understood clearly it becomes a source of power. Because your actions have consequences and those consequences affect the whole systems around you, you can choose how your actions shape those systems, and the

results will inevitably cycle back into your own life. All seven of the laws, as we will see, are sources of power in this way. As you learn to work with them, you will find that you can change your life and your surroundings in ways you cannot yet imagine.

Awareness exercise

During the week you spend on this lesson, as you go about your daily activities, think about the Law of Wholeness and apply it to the things you encounter over the course of the day. Pay attention to those things and people that move in harmony with the Law, and see how they benefit from it; pay attention to those things and people who seem to conflict with the law, and see if you can figure out how this happens and what the consequences will be.

Affirmation

"In all that I am and all that I do—I am part of a greater whole."

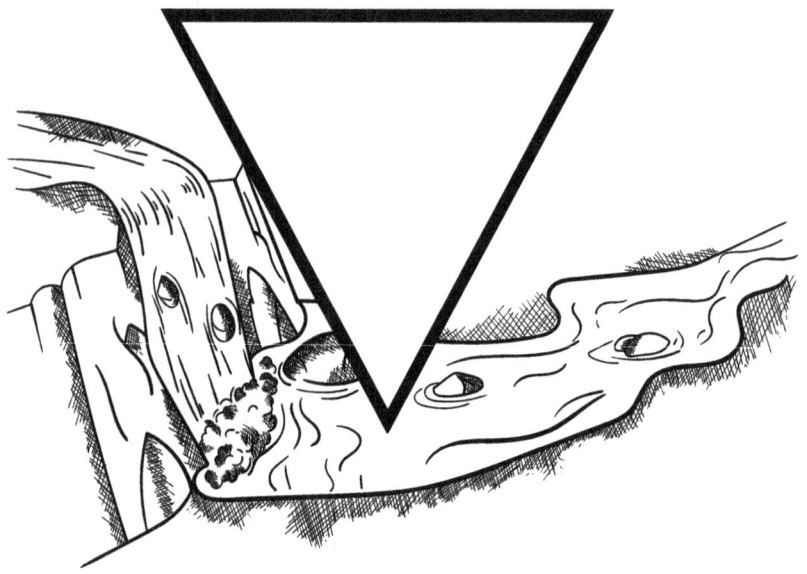

The second law, the Law of Flow, warns against trying to treat anything in the Cosmos as a static, permanent, unchanging reality. Everything flows into being and back out of being, and everything is supported by flows from other things and supports other things in turn by what flows out from it. Real prosperity is not a matter of clinging to accumulation but of being able to tap into abundant flows, and contribute to them in turn.

LESSON 42

The law of flow

1. The Law of Wholeness provides the background for the other six laws that will be discussed here. It shows that the cosmos is best understood as a whole system, a single phenomenon in which everything is part of everything else. It is important to realize, however, that the cosmos is not static. It is in constant motion in all its parts, and its motions follow a law of their own, which is the Law of Flow.
2. The Law of Flow can be expressed as follows: "Everything that exists is created and sustained by flows of matter, energy, and information that come from the whole system to which it belongs, and return to that whole system. Participating in these flows, without interfering with them, brings health and wholeness; blocking them, in an attempt to turn flows into accumulations, causes suffering and disruption to the whole system and all its parts."
3. At our current stage of spiritual evolution, it can sometimes be difficult for us to notice the reality of flow in the world around us, and the habitual thoughts of our culture add to this difficulty. Our minds assign the various inputs they receive from the senses into categories with definite boundaries—this is a dog, that is a cat, and so on. In the Western world, our languages encourage this sort of thinking by

putting so much stress on nouns such as "dog" and "cat." That habit of speech and thought leads us to think of the patterns that we experience around us as a collection of separate, enduring things with unchanging definitions.

4. Look more closely, however, and those rigid categories dissolve into flow. The dog who sits by your chair, looking up at you and wondering why you are reading this lesson instead of throwing a ball for him to catch, is a flowing shape that begins as a blind, tiny puppy and ends as an old gray dog huddled in a warm place. The entire species of dogs is another flowing shape that began when certain groups of humans and wolves worked out an uneasy coexistence far back in the Stone Age, and is moving onward through all the present breeds and forms and activities of dogs into an unknown future. Other flowing shapes interact with the individual dog and the species of dogs, forming part of the broader flow of life itself.

5. You are also a flowing shape. Your material body traces out one path of flow that leads from birth to death, and your other bodies have their own currents of movement from their beginnings to their ends. Meanwhile all of humanity traces out another path that leads from the origin of our species to its extinction sometime in the unknown future, while your soul, and the swarm of souls to which it belongs, follows a vaster path that begins in the deeps of time and will end in the unimaginably far future, when we become the Lords of Freedom and take our destined place in the mighty dance of created beings that is the solar system.

6. The crucial point in dealing with all these patterns of movement is that they function best when they are allowed to move freely. Our culture glorifies mindless accumulation—"he who dies with the most toys, wins"—and that unhelpful habit encourages people to try to raise barriers in the path of the natural flow of events so they can cling to this or that product of flow. This never ends well, because accumulation chokes off flow and brings illness of one sort or another, depending on the plane where it occurs. Nor can flow be stopped forever; as another saying has it, "he who dies with the most toys, still dies."

7. To understand the nature of flow is to gain another of the secrets of power. Once you understand that you can never really hold onto anything, that you are a flowing shape in constant transformation and so are all the other beings and things with which you interact,

you can learn to work with flow, to let the things you want to release from your life flow away from you, while learning how to make the things you want to bring into your life flow toward you. Like the surfer poised on the curling wave or the sailor spreading canvas before the wind, you can then learn to let the greater flows of the cosmos take you where you want to go.

Awareness exercise

During the week you spend on this lesson, as you go about your daily activities, think about the Law of Flow and apply it to the things you encounter over the course of the day. Pay attention to those things and people that move in harmony with the Law, and see how they benefit from it; pay attention to those things and people who seem to conflict with the law, and see if you can figure out how this happens and what the consequences will be.

Affirmation

"What I receive from the universe—depends on what I give to the universe."

The third law, the Law of Balance, reminds us that everything in the Cosmos is like a pendulum; every movement one way will inevitably be balanced by a movement the other way. The balance of the Cosmos is a source of suffering for those who ignore it but becomes a source of great strength for those who understand how to use it, and ride the movements of balance the way a surfer rides a wave.

LESSON 43

The law of balance

1. Wholeness and flow provide the basic framework of the cosmos at every level. As we study the things that happen to us and around us, however, other principles become visible, and one of them is the principle of balance. When things flow in one direction, sooner or later they will flow back in the other direction. East Asian cultures have symbolized this for countless centuries with the symbolism of yin and yang, but it is an insight found in every occult and spiritual tradition and it guides effective action in every aspect of life.
2. The Law of Balance can be expressed as follows: "Everything that exists can continue to exist only by being in balance with itself, with other things, and with the whole system of which it is a part. That balance is not found by going to one or the other extreme, or by remaining fixed at a static point; it is created by self-correcting movements to either side of a midpoint."
3. This law, too, is sometimes difficult for us to grasp at our current state of spiritual evolution, and especially so in terms of the habitual thoughts of our culture. It can be hard to realize that too much really can be as bad as not enough, and that trying to push things all the way to one extreme simply guarantees that sooner or later they will

swing all the way back to the other extreme. Yet this is what experience teaches. Think back over your own life and you will be able to find many examples of the Law of Balance at work. Look at the future ahead of you and you may be able to glimpse ways that you can use this law for your benefit.

4. One of the things that makes this law difficult to understand is the habit of thinking of a good thing as the opposite of a bad thing. If you think this way, it is understandable that you would try to go to the good extreme all the time! A good thing, however, is not the opposite of one bad thing but the midpoint between two bad things, and the opposite of one bad idea is usually another bad idea. Just as staying properly hydrated puts you at a point that is halfway between drowning and dying of thirst, and a good meal is halfway between too little food and too much, everything that makes life worth living is a midpoint between two equally miserable extremes. Grasp this application of the Law of Balance and you will escape from a trap that ruins many lives.

5. As you think about the Law of Balance, be careful not to make the mistake of imagining it as static and unmoving. As the Law of Flow teaches, the whole cosmos is in motion, and so is every part of it. Balance in a universe of flow is expressed through constant adjustments. Think of a bicycle rider in motion: the weight of the rider shifts fractionally from side to side so that the bicycle remains upright. That same kind of balance in motion is present in all things and at all times.

6. Since your own actions influence the balance of your life, you can use the Law of Balance intentionally by making use of the principle of the rebound. If you need to move things one way in your life, start by moving them the opposite direction, and then ride the return swing the way you want to go. You do this whenever you practice meditation: spending a few minutes each morning withdrawing into yourself, in silence and stillness, makes it easier for you to go out into the world and encounter life fully. The same principle can be applied in many other ways.

7. Thus the Law of Balance is another of the secret keys of power. If you understand that everything in the cosmos is in balance, and know that movement one way will always be balanced by movement the other way, you can watch the pendulum swing of events and time your own decisions to take advantage of reversals and

balancing movements that most people never saw coming. You can make changes in your own life to come into balance with yourself and your surroundings, and you can use the principle of rebound to move yourself in directions that you want to go.

Awareness exercise

During the week you spend on this lesson, as you go about your daily activities, think about the Law of Balance and apply it to the things you encounter over the course of the day. Pay attention to those things and people that move in harmony with this law, and see how they benefit from it; pay attention to those things and people who seem to conflict with it, and see if you can figure out how this happens and what the consequences will be.

Affirmation

"Everything that happens in my life—expresses the perfect balance of the universe."

The fourth law, the Law of Limits, is the pivot around which the other laws turn and the most important of all the keys of power. If you refuse to recognize the limits that face you in any situation, you place yourself at their mercy. If you recognize them, you can work with them, and you can overcome them by accepting other limits deliberately. Like the bones that give your muscles something to work with, limits make it possible for you to use your strength.

LESSON 44

The law of limits

1. In every set of seven laws, principles, or symbols in occult teaching, the fourth has a special role. As the central element of the sequence, it is the pivot around which the others turn, or to put the same insight in a different way, the anchor that gives the whole sequence a basis in hard fact. This is as true of the Law of Limits as it is of any other example. The Law of Limits is in many ways the most important of the seven spiritual laws discussed in this book—and it is also the least popular of them all.
2. The Law of Limits can be expressed as follows: "Everything that exists is subject to limits arising from its own nature, the nature of the whole system of which it is a part, and the nature of existence itself. Those limits are as necessary as they are inescapable, and provide the foundation for all the beauty and power each existing thing is capable of manifesting."
3. In our present culture, and in our present state of spiritual evolution, these are deeply counterintuitive thoughts. It is common in today's popular culture to think of limits in wholly negative terms, to fantasize about how wonderful it would be to be free of all limits, or even to insist that limits are always imaginary and that if you just

disbelieve in them they will go away. This is not what occult philosophy teaches, and for good reason. Consider for a moment the way that the chair you are sitting on right now limits the ability of gravity to pull you down to the floor, the way that your immune system limits the ability of microbes to infect you, and the way that your sphincters keep the contents of your bowels and bladder from getting all over everything! Even those people who claim to reject all limits depend on limits at every moment.

4. As the Law of Limits points out, limitation is the foundation of beauty. The philosopher György Doczi coined the word "dinergy" for the relationship between energy and its limits, and pointed out that it is precisely the perfect balance between energy and limitation that creates beauty. Think of a blade of grass bending in the wind: it is the dinergy, the relationship between the energy of the wind and the resilience of the grass, that creates the beauty of the curve. All human arts and creative activities, similarly, use the relationship between energy and limits as an essential principle to bring beauty into manifestation.

5. This law also points out that limitation is the foundation of power. This can be seen even in the most material contexts. Like a runner whose feet push against the blocks at the beginning of a sprint, every action depends on resistance to gain power; your muscles can move your body because your skeleton gives them a limitation to work against, just as a sail offers resistance to the wind and therefore sets a sailboat skimming across the waves. The more tightly you limit the flow of energy, the more forceful that flow becomes. This is among other things the secret of meditation, which focuses thoughts and thereby gives them power.

6. One way or another, you will be subject to limits. If you refuse to accept limits, then your own innate limitations or those of your circumstances will do it for you. If you deliberately accept one set of limits, on the other hand, you can often free yourself from a different set of limits. As everyone knows who has ever used a thumb to make water spray from the end of a hose, the stricter the limits you place on something, the more forcefully it will flow through the narrow space left open. This same principle can be applied to yourself, and this is one of the greatest secrets of practical occultism.

7. In previous lessons you have learned that the laws of wholeness, flow, and balance are among the secret keys of power. They function

in this way because they are all limitations on the free flow of energy. In the same way, the laws of cause and effect, the planes, and evolution are modes in which power can be exercised, and all of them function in this way because they, too, limit the free flow of energy. Limitation is the secret key to power, and all seven laws show you how to put that key to use. All of them are also the secret key to beauty, and your meditations can reveal to you how to put that to use as well.

Awareness exercise

During the week you spend on this lesson, as you go about your daily activities, think about the Law of Limits and apply it to the things you encounter over the course of the day. Pay attention to those things and people that move in harmony with this law, and see how they benefit from it; pay attention to those things and people who seem to conflict with it, and see if you can figure out how this happens and what the consequences will be.

Affirmation

"I embrace the limits that allow me—to manifest beauty and power in my life."

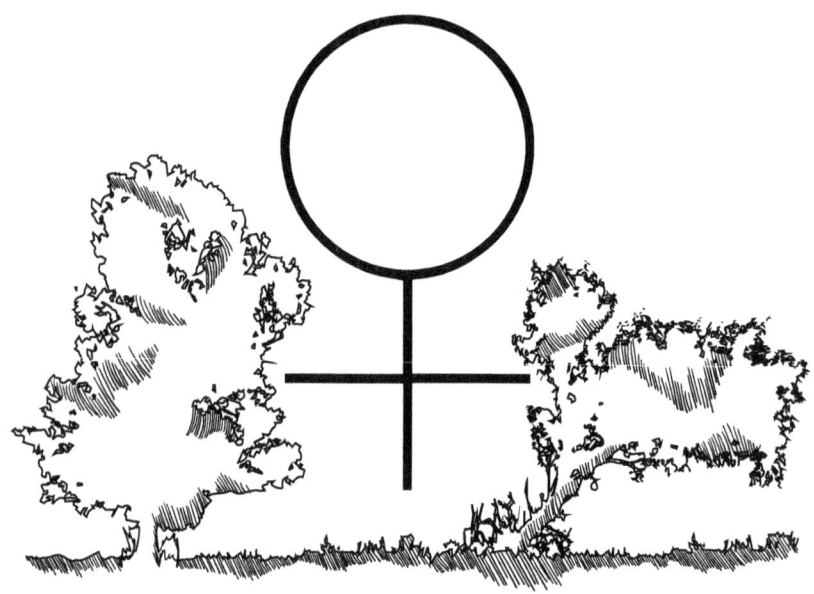

The fifth law, the Law of Cause and Effect, reminds us that everything we do has consequences and the things we desire will happen only if we set the appropriate causes into motion. Nothing in the Cosmos happens by chance; every action is a seed from which a tree will rise, spreading seeds of its own in due course.. While our ability to choose the causes that will influence us and the effects we create is far from unlimited, we always have at least some capacity to chose.

LESSON 45

The law of cause and effect

1. As you may already have noticed, there is a similarity of structure between the seven spiritual laws taught in these pages and the seven regions of each of the planes of being. The first three laws, like the lowest three regions of each plane, have the nature of substance: the laws of wholeness, flow, and balance set out the firm realities of the cosmos. The fourth law, like the fourth region of each plane, has the nature of energy: the law of limits determines what can and cannot be done in the cosmos. The last three laws, like the highest three regions of each plane, have the nature of space: they show the range of possibilities within which the potentials of the cosmos can unfold themselves. The Law of Cause and Effect is the first of the laws of space.
2. The Law of Cause and Effect can be expressed as follows: "Everything that exists is the effect of causes at work in the whole system of which each thing is a part, and becomes in turn the cause of effects elsewhere in the whole system. In these workings of cause and effect, there must always be a similarity of kind between an effect and at least one of its causes, just as there must be a similarity of scale between an effect and the sum total of its causes."

3. This law teaches that nothing anywhere in the cosmos, however great or small, takes place by what human beings like to call "chance" or "coincidence." Everything we experience is the effect of various causes, and a cause of various effects. Everything you do and everything that happens to you is influenced and set in motion by events in the past, and will influence and set in motion other events in the future. Your fate, which sums up the consequences of all your actions in previous lives, is one set of causes that affect you in this life. Your destiny, the direction in which your soul is trying to move, is another set of causes affecting you.
4. This does not mean that everything is rigidly determined in a mechanical way. The fallacy of determinism—the belief that everything that happens is predetermined by cause and effect—is just as mistaken as the corresponding fallacy of free will—the belief that cause and effect have no influence on your thoughts and actions. The truth, as usual in such cases, is in between these two extreme beliefs. In every choice you make, your fate and your destiny have a role, and so do the pressures of circumstance set in motion by chains of cause and effect in your surroundings, but you always have at least a little freedom of action, and you can expand your freedom of action by exercises that develop the will.
5. You can also learn to recognize which causes are sufficient to bring about an effect, and which are not. As this law points out, at least one of the causes of every effect must be of the same nature as the effect. What this means is that if you want something to happen on the material plane, for example, at least one of the causes you set in motion must be a material cause. You can put other causes to work on other planes to move things the way you want them to go—this is one of the secrets of magic—but along with astral or etheric factors, there must always be something material to anchor the work on the plane where you expect the effects to take shape.
6. The Law of Cause and Effect also stresses that there must always be a similarity of scale between the effect and the sum total of its causes. Can small changes cause big effects? Of course, but only when other causes of much greater scale are poised to act, and the small change is simply the one that sets all the others in motion. By itself, without the help of other factors, a small cause will only have small effects, and even a combination of powerful causes can be insufficient to cause an effect that is too large for them. It is often possible,

however, to find other forces that are already moving the way you want things to go, and add your efforts to theirs in order to achieve the results you desire.
7. The power of cause and effect in the cosmos is thus not a simple matter. Even the simplest effect is set in motion by many different causes, and even the smallest cause can combine with others to set off many different effects. The circumstances of your life are effects, and some of what has caused them is choices you have made in the past. Your will is a cause, and it will have some influence on the circumstances of your life in times to come.

Awareness exercise

During the week you spend on this lesson, as you go about your daily activities, think about the Law of Cause and Effect and apply it to the things you encounter over the course of the day. Pay attention to those things and people that move in harmony with this law, and see how they benefit from it; pay attention to those things and people who seem to conflict with it, and see if you can figure out how this happens and what the consequences will be.

Affirmation

"Everything I experience is the effect of causes in the past—and everything I do will be the cause of effects in the future."

The sixth law is the Law of the Planes, which reminds us that the world of dense matter we experience with our senses is not the only world we inhabit—much less the only world that matters to us. To recognize the world around us as a place where many planes interact is an important step toward wisdom. More important still is to come to know ourselves as beings who dwell at once on several planes.

LESSON 46

The law of the planes

1. Much of this book has been devoted to an exploration of the planes of being, and long before you reached this lesson you had at least some understanding of the four planes on which human beings can act at this stage in their evolution: the material plane, the etheric plane, the astral plane, and the mental plane. That knowledge is an essential foundation for every aspect of occult study and practice, and this law is among other things a reminder of the practical importance of that knowledge.
2. The Law of the Planes can be expressed as follows: "Everything that exists, exists and functions on one of several planes of being, or is composed of things from more than one plane acting together as a whole system. These planes are discrete, not continuous, and the passage of influences from one plane to another can only take place under conditions defined by the relationship of the planes involved."
3. The maxim that the planes of being are discrete and not continuous is among the most important things you have been taught in this course. The mistaken assumption that what is true on one plane must be true on another is a source of many costly errors, as when people think that an idea that is emotionally appealing (and thus effective on the

astral plane) must therefore also be practically workable (and thus effective on the material plane). The capable occultist understands the difficulties with this way of thinking, recognizes that each plane has its own laws and principles, which cannot be ignored with impunity, and acts on each plane in the ways appropriate to that plane.

4. While the planes are discrete, and the influences of one plane do not necessarily pass to other planes, there are points of contact that link planes that are (metaphorically) next to each other. Thus the material plane and the etheric plane have points of contact, so do the etheric and astral planes, and so do the astral and mental planes. When one or more planes come between a pair of planes, it is necessary to work through the intervening plane or planes to move a pattern of forces from one to the other. Thus, for example, to bring an influence from the astral plane down into manifestation in the material plane, you must treat the etheric plane as a bridge, making use of one point of contact to bring the influence from the astral to the etheric plane, and another to bring it from the etheric to the material plane.

5. Complicated as this seems, interaction across the boundaries of the planes happens all the time. As was pointed out in an early lesson in this book, you yourself are an example of a point of contact among the planes. Every time you move your body, after all, your intention passes from the astral plane where it was formulated, through the etheric plane, to result in action on the material plane. As the Law of the Planes points out, there are whole systems that include elements from two or more planes, and again, you are one of these. Whole systems composed of factors from several planes are among the most recognizable points of contact between planes, and your material, etheric, and astral bodies, and mental sheath, embody the points of contact among planes that are most readily accessible to you.

6. This is why so much occult study and practice focuses on the goal of self-knowledge. To know yourself is among other things to understand how the planes interact in you, and to know how to move influences up and down from plane to plane at will. That knowledge makes it possible for you to work with your own body and mind in ways that are closed to most people, but it also opens the way to learning how to do this with other points of contact among planes, whether those are embodied as human beings or otherwise. That way lies immense power, though it also involves grave responsibilities.

7. The attainment of the goals of occultism—wisdom, revelation, and enlightenment—is the most important, as well as the most challenging, of the many applications of the Law of the Planes. To gain wisdom is to find the points of contact within yourself that link the astral plane to the mental plane, and begin to draw down influences from the mental plane into your own thoughts and feelings. To experience revelation is to open those points of contact wide, so that you can perceive the mental plane directly at least for a moment, and to attain enlightenment is to establish the free flow of influences through those points of contact, so that wisdom and revelation become constant conditions of the soul.

Awareness exercise

During the week you spend on this lesson, as you go about your daily activities, think about the Law of the Planes and apply it to the things you encounter over the course of the day. Pay attention to those things and people that move in harmony with this law, and see how they benefit from it; pay attention to those things and people who seem to conflict with it, and see if you can figure out how this happens and what the consequences will be.

Affirmation

"I respond to each reality I encounter—on its appropriate plane."

The seventh law, the Law of Evolution, completes the sequence of seven laws and leads beyond it. It reminds us that our current condition is temporary, part of the vast evolutionary journey that is leading each of us through life after life toward destinies greater than we can imagine. In a very important sense, we are unfinished, and the work of occult study and practice—the work of the narrow, hidden path—leads in the direction of those destinies.

LESSON 47

The law of evolution

1. In every set of seven things found in occult philosophy, whether we are discussing regions of the planes or laws of the cosmos, the seventh represents both the completion of the sequence and the transition to something beyond it. The seventh of the spiritual laws discussed here, the Law of Evolution, is no exception to that rule. You have already learned a great deal about evolution in the lessons in this book. To understand the Law of Evolution is to understand the context of all of the other laws—and to begin to glimpse where the seven laws lead.
2. The Law of Evolution can be expressed as follows: "Everything that exists comes into being by a process of evolution that starts with adaptation to changing conditions and ends by establishing a steady state in balance with its surroundings, following a threefold rhythm of challenge, response, and reintegration. Evolution is gradual rather than sudden, and it works by increasing diversity and accumulating possibilities, rather than following a predetermined line of development."
3. It is difficult to name another idea that has been misunderstood as thoroughly as evolution. Evolution is not the same thing as

improvement—it does not necessarily make things better over time. Evolution is not the same thing as progress—it does not necessarily move in any one direction, or in any direction at all. Evolution is not the same thing as hierarchy—nothing is "more evolved" than anything else, since everything that exists today has been evolving for the same immense period of time. Evolution is adaptation. It is the process by which beings adapt themselves to changing environments, and change as a result.

4. The process of evolution begins when a being or a group of beings has to deal with a change in their environment. That challenge calls forth a variety of responses, some of which are more successful than others. Those that are successful lead the being or the group of beings who make those responses into a new relationship to the environment, opening up new possibilities and closing off old ones. That new relationship then settles down into a stable condition, which lasts until the next challenge arises and sets the evolutionary process in motion again.

5. Every living thing is what it is today because its ancestors responded to a changing environment by trying something new, and succeeding. The distant ancestors of the cat family, for example, explored different ways of survival; some chased larger prey, some smaller; over countless ages, genetic adaptations took place, and the descendants of those ancient animals are now lions, tigers, jaguars, cheetahs, lynxes, bobcats, house cats, and all the other kinds of cats that exist today. In the far future, millions of years from now, some of those lineages will no longer exist while others will have taken on new forms, because new challenges will arise and new adaptations will emerge in response.

6. This is as true of spiritual evolution as it is of biological evolution. When your soul first became human, for example, it entered into a new environment with many new challenges. Your first rudimentary mental sheath put you in contact with a new world of meaning, while the loss of guidance from an animal group soul left you without a familiar source of guidance. Since that time, in life after life, you have adapted to those changes in various ways, some successful, some less so. Once you have finished adapting to the problems and possibilities of the human kingdom, in turn, you can expect a new round of challenges to open up as spiritual evolution takes you to the next stage of your journey.

7. That journey does not lead you to a predetermined end. Rather, the point of the process of evolution is to unfold the potentials of your soul in a unique way. When you began your ascent through the planes in the mineral kingdom, you were identical to every other soul at that same stage, but every experience you have had since then has made you at least a little different from other souls. Now, as a human being, you have become even more of an individual, and the path ahead of you will lead you in unique directions. It is for this reason that in some occult schools, the title given to initiates of the highest degree is *Ipsissimus*—a Latin word that means "most completely oneself."

Awareness exercise

During the week you spend on this lesson, as you go about your daily activities, think about the Law of Evolution and apply it to the things you encounter over the course of the day. Pay attention to those things and people that move in harmony with this law, and see how they benefit from it; pay attention to those things and people who seem to conflict with it, and see if you can figure out how this happens and what the consequences will be.

Affirmation

"Together with all other beings—I am part of the evolutionary process."

This course is a portal to a wider world. As a student of these lessons, you have learned some of the basic concepts of occult philosophy, and if you have practiced the meditations and other spiritual exercises that accompany the lessons, you have also begun to develop certain skills you can use to proceed further in occultism. Whether you pass through that portal, of course, you and you alone can decide.

LESSON 48

The work of the occultist

1. Over the year that you have just spent working on the lessons in this book, you have been introduced to some of the basic concepts of occult philosophy. If you have also explored these lessons in your daily meditations, and practiced the awareness exercises and affirmations given in these pages, you have worked with these same concepts using your subjective mind as well as your objective mind. These are significant first steps in your training as an occultist. It is important to realize, however, that they are first steps, and that their value depends on what you do with them as you proceed.
2. Occult teachings can be approached simply as a collection of curious theories about yourself and the cosmos. Even if this is all you do with them, they have a definite value. They will help you make sense of aspects of your experience that the conventional wisdom of our time fails to explain, and they will give you practical guidance in dealing with the subtler phases of human experience. Approach yourself and your life on the basis of these theories and you will find that they provide perspectives that will help in many ways, some of them unexpected.

3. As the Introduction to this book explains, however, this sort of general education is not the central purpose of the lessons you have just read. Their primary goal is to train your mind, so that you learn to think in ways that were probably unfamiliar to you before you started this course of study. They have been designed to help you develop the mental skills essential to your further work as an occultist. If you have studied the teachings with this in mind, and worked with them in meditation and other occult practices, you will have made a significant start in the quest for wisdom that is central to occult training.

4. The question before you at this point is what you will do next, now that you have devoted a year to the course of study presented in this book. You and you alone can answer that question. If you are a student of the Golden Section Fellowship, the tradition of occultism for which this book was written, the practices you have already learned are sufficient for a lifetime but you will need more raw material for your meditations and your studies. If you are a student of a different school of occultism, or if this book is your first introduction to occult study and practice, the same thing will be true for you sooner or later.

5. The first task of an occultist in training, after taking up a set of occult practices and making them part of your daily routine, is to get a good grounding in the basic elements of occult philosophy. These lessons are meant to provide that. You may find, however, that you want to know more about some aspect of the teachings presented here; you may want to see what other schools of occultism have to say about the same matters, or about subjects not covered in this book; or you may simply find that occult philosophy fascinates you and you want to learn more about it. There are many books you can use as resources for further study and meditation on these subjects; some are listed in the bibliography of this book.

6. Once you have a firm grasp of the basic elements of occult philosophy, you may find it useful to expand your field of knowledge and begin to explore the relation of occultism to other fields of knowledge. In the Golden Section Fellowship, the study of sacred geometry and its sister art of astrology are particularly recommended for this stage of the work, but there are many other branches of study that can be brought into contact with occultism, ranging from mythology and folklore to the natural sciences. It is important to pay attention to your own interests here, for you will learn best if you pursue the things that inspire and fascinate you.

7. To learn wisdom and to seek wisdom are thus central themes of the work of the occultist, but there is a third theme to keep in mind: to enact wisdom, to do what is wise in your own life and in the world as a whole. The primary work of occult training—the *ergon*, as it was called by occultists in centuries past—is to complete the work of personal evolution on the human level and awaken to the mental plane. Alongside this central focus, however, is the *parergon* or secondary work of making the world a better place for all. How you do this is up to you; different people have different talents and interests, and the *parergon* suited to one is rarely suited to another. It is still wise to remember that the work you do as an occultist is not for yourself alone, but for all humanity and all beings everywhere.

Awareness exercise

During the week you spend on this lesson, take some time to think back over everything you have learned from this book over the course of the year now ending. You may find it useful to glance back over the previous lessons, and to look over your practice journal if you kept one. What have you learned from the work you have done with this book? What do you want to learn next?

Affirmation

"The visible and invisible worlds—transform each other in me."

ADDITIONAL LESSONS

THE FOUR GATES OF THE YEAR

Preliminary note

As mentioned in the Introduction, the following lessons are meant to be studied, and used as themes for meditation and practice, during the weeks when the equinoxes and solstices take place. It does not matter where you are in the main sequence of lessons; simply postpone the next lesson in the sequence for a week, do the lesson for the solstice or equinox that week, and then pick up again with the lesson you would have done.

The additional lessons contain a certain amount of repetition. This is deliberate, partly because they are studied at three-month intervals and some of the details are likely to get lost over that time, partly because these meditations serve the same function as seasonal rituals, which are also repetitive in nature. Since the point of this book is to train the mind rather than simply to fill it with information, the carefully timed repetition of certain concepts will help the student attune to the energies of the seasons on several levels.

The spring equinox, one of the four gates of the year in occult tradition, corresponds to the element of air, to the astral plane, and to the fifth region of every plane. It begins a season of increased creative energy and emotional intensity, and its keynote is Life.

ADDITIONAL LESSON 1

The spring equinox

1. The four stations of the year have been important times for occultists for many thousands of years. Each of those stations are defined by the apparent movements of the Sun in Earth's sky. On the day of the spring equinox, everywhere on Earth between the arctic and antarctic circles, the Sun rises due east and sets due west. This is one of the two points of perfect balance in the circle of the year, where day and night are of equal length, and the subtle influences of Sun and Earth are in harmony.
2. Each station of the year is assigned to one of the four elements of ancient science and occult philosophy, and the element assigned to the spring equinox is air. This element is not the mix of material substances we call "air" but a principle that is present on all the planes of being. Each of the elements has a close connection to one of the four lowest planes of being, however, and the element of air has its connection with the astral plane, the fifth plane of being. This is the plane most strongly affected by the coming of spring.
3. At the time of the spring equinox, on or around 21 March in the northern hemisphere and 22 September in the southern hemisphere, the Earth's astral body thus receives an influx of energy from the

Sun. The northern and southern halves of the planet receive that current of energy in alternation; every six months, one receives it and the other receives its equal and opposite force, the current of the autumn equinox.

4. The fifth region of each plane of being, from the material plane to the divine plane, is also linked to the element of air. On the material plane, the fifth region is the region of gases, including those that make up our atmosphere. On the etheric plane, the fifth region is the highest of the chemical ethers; on the astral plane, it is the realm of individual likes and dislikes; on the mental plane, it is the realm of functions. The forms taken by the element of air on the planes above the mental plane are beyond our understanding at this stage of our evolution.

5. The keynote of this gate of the year in occult tradition is said to be Life. This is why so many flowers bloom and so many animals have their mating or birthing seasons in the spring, and why many people can feel the energies of life more strongly in the spring than at any other time of the year. While the life force itself belongs to the etheric plane, the ability to sense it and respond to it consciously is a function of the astral plane, and the astral plane is also the realm of the forms and colors that descend to the physical plane in the form of flowers in the plant kingdom, mating activities in the animal kingdom, and the stimulation of the emotional nature in the human kingdom.

6. Five thousand years ago Aldebaran, one of the four royal stars, the brightest star in the constellation Taurus, marked the place of the Sun among the stars at the time of the spring equinox. The shifting of the great rays of the cosmos, which is echoed in the slow movement of the heavens called the precession of the equinoxes, removed Aldebaran from that position long ago. In the present age of the world, the age of Aquarius, the royal star Fomalhaut marks the position of the Sun at the spring equinox, and it is the guardian star of this gate of the year. Traditionally the four royal stars mark the gates through which the Star Logoi send their influences down to the Earth to join with the energies from the Solar Logos.

7. Whether you celebrate this station of the year with ritual or simply use the methods of meditation to explore its significance and attune with its energies, it can be helpful to imagine the gate of the spring equinox set among the stars in the eastern sky. During the week you spend on this lesson, at the beginning of each of your

daily meditations, build up that image in your imagination, and then imagine the gate opening to release a great current of Life that flows out upon the Earth. If the traditions you follow assign that quarter of the world to a god or an angel, be aware of the presence of that being in the East, and consider saying a brief prayer. This is a sacred time to occultists, and it is well to acknowledge that.

Awareness exercise

During the week you spend on this lesson, as you go about your daily activities, pay attention to the astral plane and the fifth region of the other planes, and see if you can notice the shifts taking place in them as the new season begins. Imagine the first of the star gates opening to send its influence down to Earth, and make an effort to attune yourself to the force of Life.

Affirmation

"In this time of mingled powers—I align myself with the life of the cosmos."

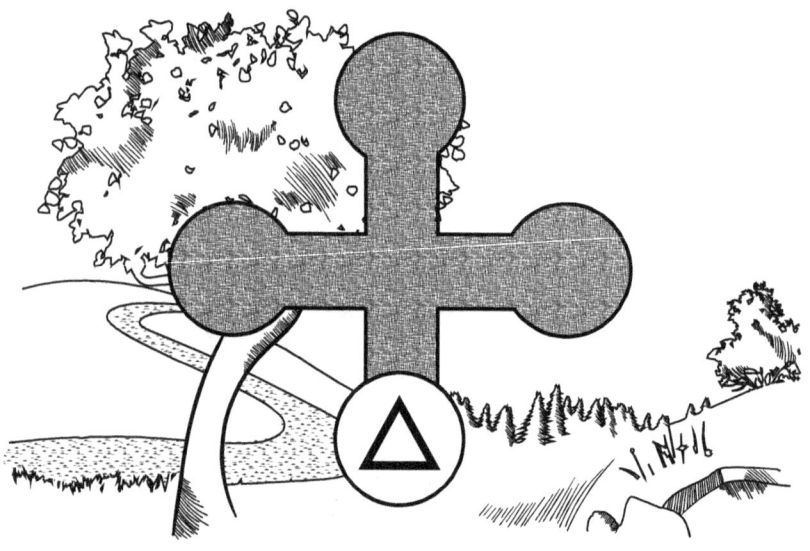

The summer solstice, one of the four gates of the year in occult tradition, corresponds to the element of fire, to the mental plane, and to the fourth region of every plane. It begins a season of increased opportunity for revelation and enlightenment, and its keynote is Light.

ADDITIONAL LESSON 2

The summer solstice

1. The four stations of the year have been important times for occultists for many thousands of years. Each of those stations are defined by the apparent movements of the Sun in Earth's sky. At the summer solstice in the northern hemisphere, the Sun rises and sets further north than at any other time; in the southern hemisphere, it rises and sets further south. This is a time of extremes, when the light ethers of the solar current are at their strongest and the chemical ethers of the telluric current at their weakest.
2. Each station of the year is assigned to one of the four elements of ancient science and occult philosophy, and the element assigned to the summer solstice is fire. This element is not the chemical reaction we call "fire" but a principle that is present on all the planes of being. Each of the elements has a close connection to one of the four lowest planes of being, however, and the element of fire has its connection with the mental plane, the fourth plane of being. This is the plane most strongly affected by the arrival of midsummer.
3. At the time of the summer solstice, on or around 22 June in the northern hemisphere and 21 December in the southern hemisphere, the solar current thus descends most strongly to the Earth and the

mental body of the Earth is strongly affected by it. The northern and southern halves of the planet receive this descent of force in alternation; every six months, one receives it and the other receives its equal and opposite force, the upward flow of the telluric current at the winter solstice.

4. The fourth region of each plane, from the material plane to the divine plane, is also linked to the element of fire. On the material plane, the fourth region is the region of energy, including the light and heat emitted by flame. On the etheric plane, the fourth region is the life ether; on the astral plane, it is the realm of interest and indifference; on the mental plane, it is the realm of reflective consciousness. The forms taken by the element of fire on the planes above the mental plane are beyond our understanding at this stage of our evolution.

5. The keynote of this gate of the year in occult tradition is said to be Light. This has an obvious expression in the bright days of summer, when the Sun rises higher in the heavens and stays up longer than at any other time, but it also refers to the light of consciousness and meaning, the keynote of the mental plane. It is for this reason that many religions and occult schools celebrate a holy day related to enlightenment or inspiration on or near the summer solstice. Pentecost is an example from the Christian tradition; the rite welcoming the summer solstice at Stonehenge is an example from the Druid tradition.

6. Five thousand years ago Regulus, one of the four royal stars, the brightest star in the constellation Leo, marked the place of the Sun among the stars at the time of the summer solstice The shifting of the great rays of the cosmos, which is echoed in the slow movement of the heavens called the precession of the equinoxes, removed Regulus from that position long ago. In the present age of the world, the age of Aquarius, the royal star Aldebaran marks the position of the Sun at the summer solstice, and it is the guardian star of this gate of the year. Traditionally the four royal stars mark the gates through which the Star Logoi send their influences down to the Earth to join with the energies from the Solar Logos.

7. Whether you celebrate this station of the year with ritual or simply use the methods of meditation to explore its significance and attune with its energies, it can be helpful to imagine the gate of the summer solstice set among the stars in the southern sky. During the week you spend on this lesson, at the beginning of each of your daily

meditations, build up that image in your imagination, and then imagine the gate opening to release a great current of Light that flows out upon the Earth. If the traditions you follow assign that quarter of the world to a god or an angel, be aware of the presence of that being in the South, and consider saying a brief prayer. This is a sacred time to occultists, and it is well to acknowledge that.

Awareness exercise

During the week you spend on this lesson, as you go about your daily activities, pay attention to the mental plane and the fourth region of the other planes, and see if you can notice the shifts taking place in them as the new season begins. Imagine the second of the star gates opening to send its influence down to Earth, and make an effort to attune yourself to the force of Light.

Affirmation

"In this time of powers in polarity—I align myself with the light of the cosmos."

The autumn equinox, one of the four gates of the year in occult tradition, corresponds to the element of water, to the etheric plane, and to the sixth region of every plane. It begins a season of gathering together of the life force in response to the coming of winter, and its keynote is Love.

ADDITIONAL LESSON 3

The autumn equinox

1. The four stations of the year have been important times for occultists for many thousands of years. Each of those stations are defined by the apparent movements of the Sun in Earth's sky. On the day of the autumn equinox, everywhere on Earth between the arctic and antarctic circles, the Sun rises due east and sets due west. This is one of the two points of perfect balance in the circle of the year, where day and night are of equal length, and the subtle influences of Sun and Earth are in harmony.
2. Each station of the year is assigned to one of the four elements of ancient science and occult philosophy, and the element assigned to the autumn equinox is water. This element is not the chemical compound we call "water" but a principle that is present on all the planes of being. Each of the elements has a close connection to one of the four lowest planes of being, however, and the element of water has its connection with the etheric plane, the sixth plane of being. This is the plane most strongly affected by the coming of autumn.
3. At the time of the autumn equinox, on or around 22 September in the northern hemisphere and 21 March in the southern hemisphere, the etheric body of the Earth thus receives an influx of energy from

the Sun. The northern and southern halves of the planet receive that current of energy in alternation; every six months, one receives it and the other receives its equal and opposite force, the current of the spring equinox.
4. The sixth region of each plane, from the material plane to the divine plane, is also linked to the element of water. On the material plane, the sixth region is the region of liquids, of which chemical water is the most common on our world. On the etheric plane, the sixth region is the middlemost of the chemical ethers; on the astral plane, it is the realm influenced by the thoughts and ideas of others; on the mental plane, it is the realm of names. The forms taken by the element of water on the planes above the mental plane are beyond our understanding at this stage of our evolution.
5. The keynote of this gate of the year in occult tradition is said to be Love. This should not be understood in a purely romantic sense, much less a purely sexual one; every form of love, especially the love of family members and friends for each other and the love of human beings for deity, is heightened at this season. The connections on the etheric plane that bind us together are strengthened by the mingled energies of Sun and Earth at this season, as the Sun passes the midpoint in its journey toward winter.
6. Five thousand years ago Antares, one of the four royal stars, the brightest star in the constellation Scorpio, marked the place of the Sun among the stars at the time of the autumn equinox. The shifting of the great rays of the cosmos, which is echoed in the slow movement of the heavens called the precession of the equinoxes, removed Antares from that position long ago. In the present age of the world, the age of Aquarius, the royal star Regulus marks the position of the Sun at the autumn equinox, and it is the guardian star of this gate of the year. Traditionally the four royal stars mark the gates through which the Star Logoi send their influences down to the Earth to join with the energies from the Solar Logos.
7. Whether you celebrate this station of the year with ritual or simply use the methods of meditation to explore its significance and attune with its energies, it can be helpful to imagine the gate of the autumn equinox set among the stars in the western sky. During the week you spend on this lesson, at the beginning of each of your daily meditations, build up that image in your imagination, and then imagine the gate opening to release a great current of Love that flows out

upon the Earth. If the traditions you follow assign that quarter of the world to a god or an angel, be aware of the presence of that being in the West, and consider saying a brief prayer. This is a sacred time to occultists, and it is well to acknowledge that.

Awareness exercise

During the week you spend on this lesson, as you go about your daily activities, pay attention to the etheric plane and the sixth region of the other planes, and see if you can notice the shifts taking place in them as the new season begins. Imagine the third of the star gates opening to send its influence down to Earth, and make an effort to attune yourself to the force of Love.

Affirmation

"In this time of mingled powers—I align myself with the love of the cosmos."

The winter solstcie, one of the four gates of the year in occult tradition, corresponds to the element of earth, to the material plane, and to the seventh region of every plane. It begins a season of focus on material limits as a source of strength, and its keynote is Law.

ADDITIONAL LESSON 4

The winter solstice

1. The four stations of the year have been important times for occultists for many thousands of years. Each of those stations are defined by the apparent movements of the Sun in Earth's sky. At the winter solstice in the northern hemisphere, the Sun rises and sets further south than at any other time; in the southern hemisphere, it rises and sets further north. This is a time of extremes, when the light ethers of the solar current are at their weakest and the chemical ethers of the telluric current at their strongest.
2. Each station of the year is assigned to one of the four elements of ancient science and occult philosophy, and the element assigned to the winter solstice is earth. This element is not the mixture of powdered rock and organic matter we call "earth" but a principle that is present on all the planes of being. Each of the elements has a close connection to one of the four lowest planes of being, however, and the element of earth has its connection with the material plane, the seventh plane of being. This is the plane most strongly affected by the arrival of midwinter.
3. At the time of the winter solstice, on or around 21 December in the northern hemisphere and 22 June in the southern hemisphere, the

telluric current rises most strongly to the Earth's surface and the material plane is the plane of being most strongly affected by it. The northern and southern halves of the planet receive this ascending force in alternation; every six months, one receives it and the other receives its equal and opposite force, the downward flow of the solar current at the summer solstice.

4. The seventh region of each plane, from the material plane to the divine plane, is also linked to the element of earth. On the material plane, the seventh region is the region of solid matter, including the rock and soil of the earth beneath our feet. On the etheric plane, the seventh region is the densest of the chemical ethers; on the astral plane, it is the realm of biological passions; on the mental plane, it is the realm of forms. The forms taken by the element of earth on the planes above the mental plane are beyond our understanding at this stage of our evolution.

5. The keynote of this gate of the year in occult tradition is said to be Law. In winter the element of earth and the material plane are the dominant forces in life, and both of these are characterized by solidity, stability, and resistance to change. During this season life can be harsh, but the power of cosmic law also reminds us that the cycle of the seasons will continue and bring better times. It is at or near the winter solstice that many religions and occult teachings place holy days that celebrate the rebirth of light in the darkness, and this is also a function of law, an aspect of the order that holds the universe in balance.

6. Five thousand years ago Fomalhaut, one of the four royal stars, the brightest star near the constellation Aquarius, marked the place of the Sun among the stars at the time of the winter solstice. The shifting of the great rays of the cosmos, which is echoed in the slow movement of the heavens called the precession of the equinoxes, removed Fomalhaut from that position long ago. In the present age of the world, the age of Aquarius, the royal star Antares marks the position of the sun at the winter solstice, and it is the guardian star of this gate of the year. Traditionally the four royal stars mark the gates through which the Star Logoi send their influences down to the Earth to join with the energies from the Solar Logos.

7. Whether you celebrate this station of the year with ritual or simply use the methods of meditation to explore its significance and attune with its energies, it can be helpful to imagine the gate of the winter

solstice set among the stars in the northern sky. During the week you spend on this lesson, at the beginning of each of your daily meditations, build up that image in your imagination, and then imagine the gate opening to release a great current of Law that flows out upon the Earth. If the traditions you follow assign that quarter of the world to a god or an angel, be aware of the presence of that being in the North, and consider saying a brief prayer. This is a sacred time to occultists, and it is well to acknowledge that.

Awareness exercise

During the week you spend on this lesson, as you go about your daily activities, pay attention to the material plane and the seventh region of the other planes, and see if you can notice the shifts taking place in them as the new season begins. Imagine the fourth of the star gates opening to send its influence down to Earth, and make an effort to attune yourself to the force of Law.

Affirmation

"In this time of powers in polarity—I align myself with the law of the cosmos."

APPENDIX

Instructions for practice

Discursive meditation

The kind of meditation practiced in traditional Western occult schools differs in an important way from the Eastern methods of meditation commonly practiced these days. Although there are exceptions, most Eastern methods of meditation work by turning off the objective mind. In some of these kinds of meditation, students learn to fix the attention on something other than thinking—a repeated mantra, a visualization, a cycle of breathing, or bare attention itself—so that their objective minds stop thinking altogether, and deeper patterns of awareness come to the fore. Other kinds of meditation do the same thing in a subtler way, by teaching students to observe thoughts rising in the objective mind without actually thinking about them. Either of these can result in powerful spiritual experiences, but they have significant drawbacks. Shutting down the objective mind in this way too often produces people who have experienced deep spiritual states but have never learned how to think clearly, and often can't function well in everyday life.

The core traditions of Western meditation take a different path. Instead of stopping the thinking process, these methods point the focus of the objective mind on thinking itself, and turn the objective mind into a vehicle for spiritual awareness. In the standard Western method of meditation, this is done by focusing the mind on a specific topic, called a "theme", and mentally following out the implications of that theme through a chain of ideas, all the while keeping the objective mind focused on the theme. With practice, the subjective mind joins in, and begins to hand the objective mind ideas and insights it wouldn't otherwise have had, so that meditation becomes a way for your two minds to work together.

This form of meditation is called "discursive meditation", because it often takes the form of an inner discourse or dialogue. If you've practiced other kinds of meditation, discursive meditation will seem partly familiar to you and partly strange. If you've never meditated, the entire process will probably seem very strange to you! For that reason, it's best to learn discursive meditation a step at a time, beginning with posture.

To practice meditation you will need a place that is quiet and not too brightly lit. It should be private—a room with a door you can shut is best, though if you can't arrange that, a quiet corner and a little forbearance on the part of your housemates will do the job. You'll need a chair with a straight back, and a seat at a height that allows you to rest your feet flat on the floor while keeping your thighs level with the ground. You'll need a clock or watch, placed so that you can see it easily without moving your head. You'll also need this book, because the diagrams for each lesson are used in the meditation process. Once you have these simple preliminaries in place you are ready to begin.

One other detail is worth noting here. Many occult schools teach a basic ritual that is used to balance, energize, and cleanse the subtle body. In the Golden Section Fellowship, for example, the ritual used for this purpose is the Sphere of Protection. If the occult tradition you are studying includes such a ritual, it is a good idea to perform this before your meditation, so that you and the space you are in are both in a state of balance and clarity.

Posture

One of the benefits of discursive meditation is that you don't have to tie your legs into a knot to practice it. The posture to use is the one shown in any Egyptian statue of a seated god or goddess. Sit on a relatively hard chair. If it has a back, slide forward, so your back doesn't touch the chair's back at all. (This allows subtle energies to flow freely up and down your spine, which makes meditation easier.) Your feet should rest flat on the floor, your knees and hips are at right angles, your hands rest palm down on your thighs, and your head is straight. Keep your eyes open but relax your eyelids; took forward and down, as though at something on the floor a few yards ahead of you. Breathe slowly and easily.

When you're ready to practice, take this position, and don't move for five minutes. Don't fidget, shift, wiggle, scratch an itch or anything else. Leave your body completely still for five minutes by the clock. Do this once a day, preferably first thing in the morning, after your morning practice but before breakfast. Do this daily for one week.

Unless you've already done this, or practiced certain other exercises that have the same effect, this practice will be much harder than you think. Our bodies are actually full of tensions and discomforts we never notice, and part of the constant shifting and wiggling and fidgeting that most of us do most of the time is a matter of trying not to notice just how uncomfortable we are. Confront that evasion head on. Stay still for those five minutes, no matter what.

If you do that, you'll begin to learn one of the essential secrets of meditation. It is literally the most boring, grueling, frustrating thing you will ever do—and once you get the hang of how to do it and why it's important, you'll do it every day, because the benefits are worth the difficulties.

Relaxation

The second week's work is focused on relaxation. Most people these days realize that it's possible to be too tense. Since the opposite of one bad idea is generally another bad idea, it's worth remembering that it's also possible to be too relaxed. Until very recently, most people in Western societies were much too tense. It was extremely rare to encounter anyone in the Western world who was too relaxed, whose body was so lacking in tension that it was limp and floppy, and so teachers of spiritual exercises focused on relaxation. That had its effect, and now you find people on either end of the spectrum. What you find too rarely is people who have the balanced midpoint between too much tension and too much relaxation, which we can call "poise".

The practice of sitting in a fixed and slightly unnatural posture is meant to keep you from being too relaxed. Keeping the spine straight, the head held up, the legs parallel, and the body still, requires tension. Now we move to the other side of the balance and make sure you aren't too tense. This is done by relaxing your muscles while retaining the posture you've established. You don't move at all; you don't shift or wiggle or stretch; you just let go of the tensions that aren't needed to keep the posture.

Start at the crown of the head. Consciously relax any muscular tensions you find there. If you encounter a tension that won't let go, imagine that it is relaxing. (Your subjective mind will notice this, and the imagination will become reality with a little practice.) Spend a little while on that part of your body, and then move further down your head to the sides of the skull. Consciously relax any tensions you find there, if you can, and if you can't, imagine the tensions dissolving. Take this all the way down your whole body, a bit at a time, doing the same twofold relaxation on each part of your body—consciously relax what you can, and imagine the rest letting go. This should take you at least five minutes, and quite possibly more than that. All the while, maintain the seated posture without moving. Don't pay attention to your breath—that's a later phase—or to anything outside yourself; simply focus on your body, and on the process by which you're releasing unnecessary tensions.

You may find that when you finish this, you ache from head to foot, or that some part of your body hurts a little—or a lot. That's what happens when you have a lot of unnecessary tension you stopped noticing a long time ago. With repeated practice, the tension will go away. You may also find that when you finish this, some of your muscles feel as though they've had a workout. They have—you've been holding your body in an unfamiliar position for a while, and that takes muscular effort. Your body will get used to that in due time.

This is the second stage of preparation for meditation: five minutes a day, sitting motionless in a chair, relaxing your unnecessary tensions. Do this for a week before going on to the next stage.

Breathing

How you breathe has powerful effects on your state of consciousness, and there are intricate systems of breathwork that take advantage of this for various purposes. If you don't have a teacher to supervise you and watch for signs of trouble, though, those systems can be risky. Breathwork stimulates the vagus nerve, a nerve that connects the vital organs with the brain, and so has a range of effects on your nervous system and your glands; if you do intensive breathwork without supervision, as a result, you can give yourself health problems.

Fortunately there are methods of breathwork that are safe to practice on your own, and one of them is very commonly used in occult meditation. It's called "the fourfold breath." It's quite simple. You breathe in through your nose, slowly and deeply, to the count of four. You hold the breath in to the count of four. You breathe out through your nose, slowly and fully, to the count of four. You hold the breath out to the count of four. Repeat to the same steady rhythm.

How do you know how slow or fast to make the rhythm? Simply make it reasonably slow, but not so slow that you gasp or run out of air. Keep the movement of your breath steady, gentle, and flowing. No two people will have exactly the same rhythm, nor will you have the same rhythm every time you practice. Don't use a metronome or any other mechanical aid; just let yourself find a pace that works for you.

One detail worth noting is that you don't hold your breath by closing your throat; you hold it by keeping the muscles of your chest and abdomen in their positions, either expanded or relaxed. If you're used to closing your throat to hold your breath, it can take some practice to stop doing so. How do you tell if you're closing your throat? Draw in a deep breath, hold it for a little while, and then breathe out. If you hear or feel a little "pop" inside your throat, you've closed it. To avoid doing that, keep trying to breathe in a trickle of air while you hold your breath in, and keep trying to breathe out a trickle of air when you're holding your breath out. You'll get the hang of it quickly.

For the next week, five minutes of the fourfold breath will be your practice. Take the position, hold yourself still, and let the tension drain away from the crown of your head to the soles of your feet, just as you did last week. Take a minute or two to do this, then begin the fourfold breath. Keep doing it for five minutes by the clock. This is the sequence you'll use to begin the process of meditation for real next week. Keep at it, and see where it takes you.

Meditation

So far we've dealt with posture, relaxation, and breathing: the preliminaries to discursive meditation. Now it's time to go all the way and meditate. To make sense of what follows, it's important to remember that the word "meditation" literally means "thinking." (That's why we use the word "premeditated" for a crime that the perpetrator thought about before committing.) Your task in meditation is to think deliberately, seriously, and intentionally about a theme. While you work with the material in this book, the themes for your meditation are the seven paragraphs given for each lesson.

When you're ready to begin meditation, set up the diagram for the lesson you're studying so you can see it clearly from your meditation chair without turning your head. Sit down in the position we've discussed and settle into it, neither tense nor relaxed but poised. Let go of excess tension, beginning from the top of your head and letting it drain down from there; spend about a minute at that. Then do five minutes of the fourfold breath, letting your mind focus solely on your breathing. At this point you're ready to begin.

Spend a few moments looking at the diagram for the lesson, and then call to mind the paragraph on which you're going to meditate. Recall it as clearly as you can. Hold it in your mind for a little while, and then begin thinking about it.

As you do so, your thoughts will wander off the theme. Bring them back. They'll wander off again. Bring them back again. You'll have as much trouble keeping your mind on the theme as the practitioner of mind-emptying styles of meditation has keeping thoughts at bay, and you'll develop the same skills of catching your mind wandering and bringing it back to the subject of the meditation. In the intervals between these vagaries, on the other hand, you'll be learning something about the theme, and you'll also be working on the capacity for focused reflective thought, an essential human skill and one very poorly developed by most of us. Keep working on the theme for ten minutes by the clock. When you are finished, take a deep breath or two and then go on with the rest of your day.

The images for meditation are all available to download and print for personal use on the Aeon Books website or at the following URL https://www.aeonbooks.co.uk/downloads/OPWImages.pdf

Awareness exercises

In addition to the texts for meditation, each lesson includes an awareness exercise, which is meant to help focus your attention on experiences and ideas that will help you make sense of the material in the lesson. These are to be done exactly as described in the lesson. They are meant to be done in spare moments during the day, rather than at a prearranged time. If you have trouble remembering to do the awareness exercise, choose a phrase for each exercise that reminds you of the content, write it out by hand, and put the resulting note someplace where you will see it during your spare time. Once you have done this, make a habit of doing the awareness exercise as soon as you see the note, unless you have already done it that day.

Affirmations

Each lesson also includes an affirmation, which you can use to help your subjective mind begin to approach the world as an occultist does. The following practice is recommended for using the affirmations in this course:

First, every morning, when you first get out of bed, go to a window. Weather and air quality permitting, the window should be open, and it's best if sunlight comes in through the window as well. Stand facing the window.

Second, stretch, reaching up with your arms, spreading your fingers, drawing in a deep breath, and holding your body at full extension for a few moments.

Third, relax, let your arms return to your sides, and breathe out fully.

Fourth, begin breathing slowly and steadily. As you breathe in, repeat silently in your mind the first half of the affirmation for the week. Pause, retaining the breath. Then, as you breathe out, repeat silently in your mind the second half of the affirmation. Pause again, leaving the lungs empty, and repeat.

For example, with the affirmation for Lesson 1, you would silently repeat "I dwell in two worlds" while breathing in, pause, and then silently repeat "one visible and one invisible" while breathing out. There is no fixed number of repetitions for this practice, but seven deep breaths or so is a good number for most students. When you are finished, simply go on with your morning activities.

BIBLIOGRAPHY

Doczi, György (1981). *The Power of Limits*. Boston, MA: Shambhala.
Fortune, Dion (1987). *Sane Occultism*. Wellingborough, UK: Aquarian.
Fortune, Dion (2000a). *Aspects of Occultism*. York Beach, ME: Weiser.
Fortune, Dion (2000b). *The Cosmic Doctrine*. York Beach, ME: Weiser.
Greer, John Michael (2012). *Mystery Teachings from the Living Earth*. San Francisco, CA: Red Wheel/Weiser.
Greer, John Michael (2016). *The Secret of the Temple*. Woodbury, MN: Llewellyn.
Greer, John Michael (2021). *The Way of the Golden Section*. London: Aeon.
Hall, Manly Palmer (1942). *Self-Unfoldment by Disciplines of Realization*. Los Angeles, CA: Philosophical Research Society.
Hall, Manly Palmer (1982). *Man: The Grand Symbol of the Mysteries*. Los Angeles, CA: Philosophical Research Society.
Hall, Manly Palmer (1988). *Meditation Symbols in Eastern and Western Mysticism*. Los Angeles, CA: Philosophical Research Society.
Heindel, Max (1973). *The Rosicrucian Cosmo-Conception*. Oceanside, CA: Rosicrucian Fellowship.
Khei [George Winslow Plummer] (1920). *Rosicrucian Fundamentals*. New York: Flame Press.
Knight, Gareth (1997). *Occult Exercises and Practices*. Albuquerque, NM: Sun Chalice.

Michell, John (1988). *The Dimensions of Paradise*. San Francisco: Harper & Row.

Michell, John (2013). *The New View Over Atlantis*. Newburyport, MA: Hampton Roads.

Michell, John, & Allan Brown (2000). *How The World Is Made*. Rochester, VT: Inner Traditions.

Sadhu, Mouni (1959). *Concentration*. North Hollywood, CA: Wilshire.

Sadhu, Mouni (1962). *The Tarot*. North Hollywood, CA: Wilshire.

Sadhu, Mouni (2005). *Meditation: An Outline for Practical Study*. London: Aeon.

Steiner, Rudolf (1994). *How To Know Higher Worlds*. Hudson, NY: Anthroposophic Press.

Steiner, Rudolf (1995). *Intuitive Thinking as a Spiritual Path*. Hudson, NY: Anthroposophic Press.

Yeats, William Butler (1937). *A Vision*. New York, NY: Simon & Schuster.

INDEX

Aldebaran, 206, 210
animals, 12, 19–20, 23–24, 28, 35–36, 40, 43–45, 47, 62, 66, 70, 73–82, 85–86, 89, 92–94, 104, 108, 134–137, 139, 141, 194, 206
angels, 60–61, 63, 83, 98, 207, 211, 215, 219; *see also* Lords of Flame
Antares, 214, 218
Aquarius, Age of, 54, 206, 210, 214, 218
Arthur, King, 4
astral aura, 26, 28–29
astral body, 16–17, 26–33, 35, 46, 74, 77, 80, 85, 93, 96, 98, 108, 112, 119
astral double, 28
astral plane, 16–17, 27–33, 42, 46–47, 77, 82, 84, 90, 93, 108, 116, 118–121, 123
astral sheath, 28, 44, 73, 75, 94
astrology, 4, 27, 58, 198
Atlantean age, 142, 144, 154

balance, law of. *see* law of balance
beliefs, ix, 5, 33, 104, 120–121, 140, 154, 159, 186

Capricorn, Age of, 54
causal body, 16
causal plane, 14, 16, 40, 42–43, 58, 62
cause and effect, law of. *see* law of cause and effect
chemical ethers, 22–24, 48, 206, 209, 217
China, 140, 144
clairvoyance, 110, 112
cosmic planes, 52–55, 57, 165
cosmic root substance, 6, 8–12, 14–15, 43, 69, 98, 103
crystals, 19, 44, 70–71, 74

da Vinci, Leonardo, 2
dantien, 20

232 INDEX

dark matter, 54
death. *see* first death
destiny, 45, 58, 99, 105, 126–129, 131, 138, 146, 148, 186
determinism, 186
devas, 60–61, 98; *see also* Lords of Form
dinergy, 182
divine plane, 14, 16, 39–44, 47, 53, 57, 61, 65–66, 69, 97, 99, 206, 210, 214, 218
divine spark, 38, 40–41, 43, 58, 64–69, 72, 74, 76, 80, 96, 98, 126, 136, 139
Djin, 66
Doczi, György, 182
dryads, 74

Egypt, 144–145, 152, 154, 222
elementals, 64–71, 98, 134, 136, 139
enlightenment, 36, 90, 124, 159, 161, 163, 191, 208, 210
equinox, x, 202, 204–207, 210, 212–215, 218
etheric aura, 20–21, 78
etheric body, 16–21, 28, 33, 46, 70, 77, 80, 85, 93, 96–98, 112, 133
etheric double, 20, 28, 112
etheric plane, 14, 19–25, 27, 35, 42, 44, 47–48, 70, 73, 77–78, 82–84, 86–87, 90, 93, 98, 115, 122, 130, 140, 189–190, 206, 210, 212–215, 218
etheric sheath, 19–20, 44, 70–71, 74
Eurasian age, 142, 144, 146
evolution, law of. *see* law of evolution

fate, 126–129, 131–133, 138, 146, 186
first death, 110–113, 115–116, 122
Flame, Lords of. *see* Lords of Flame
flow, law of. *see* law of flow
Fomalhaut, 206, 218
Form, Lords of. *see* Lords of Form

Gaia, 58, 66
Ghob, 66
Golden Section Fellowship, 18, 198, 222

Greece, 152, 154
group souls, 72, 74–76, 78, 80, 82, 138–141, 194

hara, 20
health aura, 20
heaven, 33, 104, 118–122
hell, 33, 104, 112, 118–132
Hyperborean age, 142–143

illumination, 123, 160, 162–163
intelligences, 60–61, 63, 98; *see also* Lords of Mind
interiorization, 160, 162–163
intuition, 41, 90, 129, 159, 161–162
ipsissimus, 195

karma, 127
ki, 21

law of balance, 164, 166, 176–179
law of cause and effect, 164, 166, 184–187
law of evolution, 164, 166, 192–195
law of flow, 164, 166, 172–175, 178
law of limits, 164, 166, 180–183, 185
law of the planes, 164, 166, 188–191
law of wholeness, 164, 166, 168–171, 173
Lemurian age, 142, 144, 154
life ether, 22, 24, 48, 210
light ethers, 22, 24, 48, 209, 217
limits, law of. *see* law of limits
Lords of Flame, 60–68, 70, 74, 78, 82, 94, 98, 116
Lords of Form, 60–63, 65, 72, 74, 78, 82, 95, 98, 116
Lords of Freedom, 97–99, 112, 174
Lords of Mind, 60–63, 65, 76, 78, 82, 95, 98, 116, 153
lunar current, 25

martial arts, 21
material body, 16–18, 20, 35, 70, 73, 78, 80–81, 84–85, 93, 96–98, 103–104, 107, 112, 116, 133

material plane, 15–17, 23, 27, 42, 44, 47–48, 73, 78, 82–84, 90, 93, 97
meditation, ix, xi, 11, 13, 36–37, 48–49, 94, 124, 158, 161, 178, 182–183, 196–198, 202, 206–207, 210–211, 214, 218–219, 221–226
mental body, 16–17, 34–36, 38, 48, 80–87, 93–94, 96, 98, 112, 122, 131
mental plane, 14, 16–17, 32, 34–39, 42, 44–49, 70, 82–84, 86–87, 90, 93–94, 97–99, 104, 121–128, 130–132, 135–136, 141, 148, 159, 189, 191, 199, 206, 208–211, 214, 218
mental sheath, 16–17, 34–36, 44, 46, 48, 77, 80–87, 90, 112
meridians, 21
Mind, Lords of. *see* Lords of Mind
Moon, the, 24
Mother Nature, 58, 66
Mozart, Wolfgang A., 133

nadis, 21
nations, 90, 138–140, 153, 170
near-death experiences (NDEs), 113–117
Newton, Isaac, 4
Nichsa, 66

objective mind, 78, 81, 156–159, 161–162, 166, 197, 221–222
objective state of consciousness, 42, 44–45, 59, 66, 68–75, 77–79, 93–94, 97–98, 104, 123, 148
oreads, 74

Paralda, 66
personality, 27, 74, 104–109, 121, 124, 126–128, 156, 158, 161
pineal gland, 18
Pisces, Age of, 54
planes, law of the. *see* law of the planes
planet, 58–59, 62, 93
planetary spirit, 56–59, 55, 94, 96–97

plants, 12, 19–20, 22–24, 28, 40, 43–45, 62, 66, 70–75, 77–78, 81, 86, 92–94, 104, 108, 134, 139, 206
Polarian age, 142–143, 153
porpoises, 35, 79
prana, 21
preparation, 131, 160, 162–163, 224
Pythagoras, 154

qi, 21
quickening, 133

rays, twelve, 54, 57
Regulus, 210, 214
reincarnation, x, 103–105, 107, 130–137
Renaissance, the, 5, 152, 154
royal stars, four, 206, 210, 214, 218
Rome, 140–141, 145

second death, 114–119, 122
Seven Great Logoi, 54
silver cord, 110
solar current, 24–25, 209, 217–218
Solar Logos, 40, 56–62, 65, 74, 136, 206, 210, 214, 218
solar plexus, 18, 78
solstice, x, 202, 208–211, 216–219
spiritual body, 16, 38, 48, 96–98
spiritual plane, 14–16, 30, 38–39, 42–43, 47, 62, 94, 98
spiritual sheath, 38, 48, 97
Star Logoi, 56, 58, 65, 206, 210, 214, 218
Stonehenge, 210
subconscious mind, 158
subjective mind, 78, 81, 156–163, 166, 197, 222, 224, 227
subjective state of consciousness, 42, 44, 59, 66, 68–70, 72, 76, 78, 80
Sumer, 144
Supreme Being, 40, 52, 54, 57

Taliesin, 45
technology, 115–116, 144–145, 147
telluric current, 24–25, 209–210, 217–218

utopia, 147–148

Vitruvian man, 2

Way of the Golden Section, The, ix, xi
whales, 79
wholeness, law of. *see* law of wholeness
will, 40, 62, 98, 126–129, 136, 186–187, 190

yoga, 21

zodiac, 24, 54, 56–58

www.ingramcontent.com/pod-product-compliance
Lightning Source LLC
Chambersburg PA
CBHW061937220426
43662CB00012B/1943